THE
EHRMAN
NEEDLEPOINT
BOOK

THE
EHRMAN
NEEDLEPOINT
BOOK

Hugh Ehrman

INCLUDING DESIGNS BY
KAFFE FASSETT, CANDACE BAHOUTH
AND ELIAN McCREADY

Photography by TIM HILL
Styling by ZÖE HILL

David & Charles

A catalogue record for this book is available
from the British Library.

ISBN 0 7153 0263 9

Designed by Bridgewater Books Ltd
Photography Tim Hill
Styling Zöe Hill
Page make-up Chris Lanaway

Printed in Italy by Lego SpA
for
David & Charles
Brunel House Newton Abbot Devon

CONTENTS

INTRODUCTION

This book gathers together some of the best new work produced by Ehrman's designers over the past two or three years. It has been a wonderful book to write as I have not been restricted to a particular design theme. So often these books suffer from the self-imposed constraints of their own titles: 'Birds in Needlepoint', 'Flowers in Needlepoint', 'Geometrics' or whatever. These rather artificial classifications, dreamt up by publishers, leave the designer struggling to come up with thirty interesting, new ideas on a single subject – usually at short notice. It isn't easy and it shows. For a book to stand the test of time the quality of design needs to be consistently high and there should be variety in style and subject matter. In putting this book together I

HUGH EHRMAN IN THE LONDON SHOP, SURROUNDED
BY OLD AND NEW DESIGNS

hundred. It struck me that we had access here to some of the most interesting needlework patterns produced by some of the country's best designers over the past fifteen years. Surely it would be possible to compile a worthwhile collection of contemporary work from this lot? It certainly would be a wasted opportunity not to have a go. So, two years later here is the result.

A book is, of course, more than just a group of designs. It gives us a chance to find out more about the designers themselves and what makes them tick. Writing this book has reminded me of the wide variety of kits we produce and how much thought and effort our designers put into them. Producing over fifty new kits a year (or one a week) it is easy to lose sight of the fact that

have had a free hand in choosing from across the Ehrman range. I have been allowed to select each design purely on its own merit – a rare luxury for an author – and for this I am most grateful to my publishers, David & Charles.

When this book was first proposed my initial reaction was sceptical. Books produced by companies tend to look like glorified catalogues. Designers are better at writing about their own creations and, in any case, it is more interesting and personal to hear what they have to say themselves. It was a trip to our canvas manufacturers in Lancashire that made me think again. We were discussing how to store the stencils for all of our old designs. To my amazement I discovered that we had accumulated over four

each one is a unique creation. I sometimes think we produce too many to do justice to them all. But when our designers are in full flood it is hard to say no and at the moment they are stitching as though possessed. Creating a book gives us the chance to stand back, to take a more considered look at these designs, and to take time to appreciate detail.

The structure of the book fell happily into place. The patterns seemed to divide themselves naturally into their five groups, and the chapter headings are, I think, fairly self-explanatory. The text is intended to accompany the pictures not to intrude on them. It moves back and forth, from the specific to the general, as it makes its way along.

Whatever struck me as interesting about each particular design is what I have written about. There is background on the designers, a look at how they work, a little about the history of the source materials, and observations on colour and composition. I have tried to keep things light and to let the pictures, as far as possible, do the talking. Each design is charted with the wool quantities listed at the side. This enables colours to be changed and patterns to be altered.

When I go to trade shows abroad I am always surprised to find other British companies taking pride of place: Elizabeth Bradley, Designers' Forum, Glorafilia or Primavera outshine the local competition. There is no doubt that in this specialised area British design now leads the field and few would deny that our designers have had an important part to play in this development. It gives me a

A VIEW OF THE EHRMAN SHOP IN LONDON, WHERE
THE FULL RANGE OF NEEDLEPOINT DESIGNS
ARE ON DISPLAY

tremendous thrill that their canvases should be stitched in so many countries. I think we should be proud of them, and give credit where credit is due. We are dealing here with a genuinely talented group of people who have given enormous pleasure to thousands of stitchers around the world. I hope this book will help to illustrate the artistic regeneration that British needlework has undergone in recent years and that you will enjoy looking at their work as much as I have enjoyed writing about it.

Chapter One

~

TEXTILES

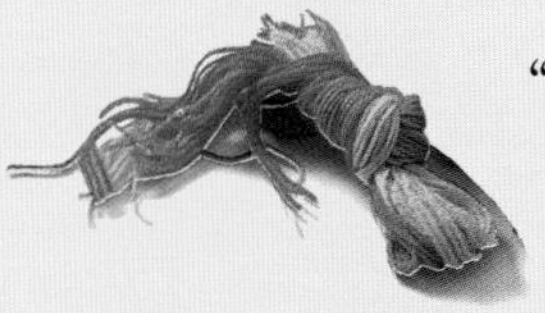

"To us pattern designers,
Persia has become a
holy-land, for there in the process of time
our art was perfected, and thence it spread to
cover for a while the world, east and west."

WILLIAM MORRIS,
THE HISTORY OF PATTERN DESIGNING.

MYSORE

This wonderful design by Annabel Nellist somehow captures a spirit of India. It is not necessarily the colours, composition or subject matter. None of these alone hold the key. A combination of these factors is partly the answer, but the extra ingredient which brings it to life is that crowded sense of Indian activity. The nature of Indian design reflects the environment of India – jostling, crowded and often chaotic. There are people everywhere. As in life, so in art – in almost all forms of Indian textile design there is movement and event, with a host of detail competing for attention. If there can be said to be one unifying feature of Indian design it would have to be 'liveliness'.

The great era of Indian textile art was under the Mughal emperors in the sixteenth century. They supervised a fusion of styles we now think of as characteristically Indian. The Mughals who ruled India from the sixteenth to the eighteenth centuries were descendants of the Mongols who, a few centuries before, had controlled Asia from east to west. With their arrival India was opened up to influences from China, Afghanistan and Persia.

It was this rich, polyglot tradition which attracted Annabel. She has chosen an unusual mixture of architecture and pattern as the subjects for her cushion cover. This surprising combination succeeds because of her sure sense of scale. The central focus of windows and roofs anchors the design which is further stabilised by a thin but strong geometric border. By using a patchwork technique the overall effect becomes more textural and less pictorial. No area of colour or pattern is allowed to dominate and as a result there is a calm sense of balance amid the profusion of detail.

AN INDIAN PATCHWORK IN WARM, CLEAN
COLOURS FROM ANNABEL NELLIST. THE COPIOUS
DETAIL CREATES THE INTEREST YET THE COMPOSITION
IS SO WELL BALANCED THAT THE OVERALL DESIGN
LOOKS QUITE RESTRAINED

Maybe this design will inspire you to try your own needle-work collage. Annabel's is a sophisticated and original design but it doesn't have to be so complicated. If you start with the regularity of a patchwork quilt you can then let discord creep in slowly! In his television programme *Glorious Colour* Kaffe Fassett showed how he sometimes developed geometric designs by playing about with groups of objects – buttons, pieces of fabric or whatever – and then seeing what patterns they fell into. I have always thought a patchwork approach to needlepoint design has tremendous possibilities. You don't need to be a great draughtsman or figurative drawer. You can start with a few relatively simple motifs and let colour and pattern do the rest. I like the way Annabel places her skyline of buildings against a backdrop of pattern. Collage is a wonderful way of superimposing unexpected images, and is great fun.

CANVAS: 12 holes to the inch

STITCH: Half-cross or tent

DESIGN AREA: 18in × 15in (48cm × 36cm)

YARN: Anchor Tapisserie or Paternayan

Shade	Anchor	Paternayan	
Flame	8204	940	5 skeins
Cream	8006	263	7 skeins
Rose Pink	8400	931	5 skeins
Ancient Blue	8744	570	4 skeins
Autumn Gold	8060	732	3 skeins
Cinnamon	9384	443	8 skeins
Ocean Blue	8838	531	2 skeins
Gobelin Green	8882	532	3 skeins
Cherry Red	8220	900	5 skeins
Maize	8040	753	2 skeins

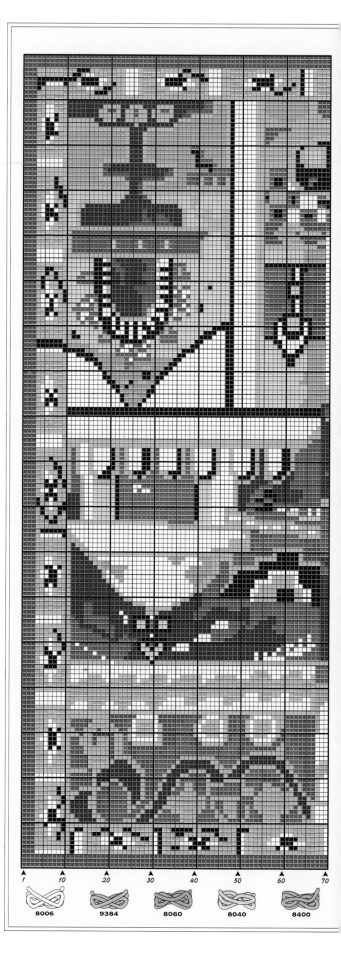

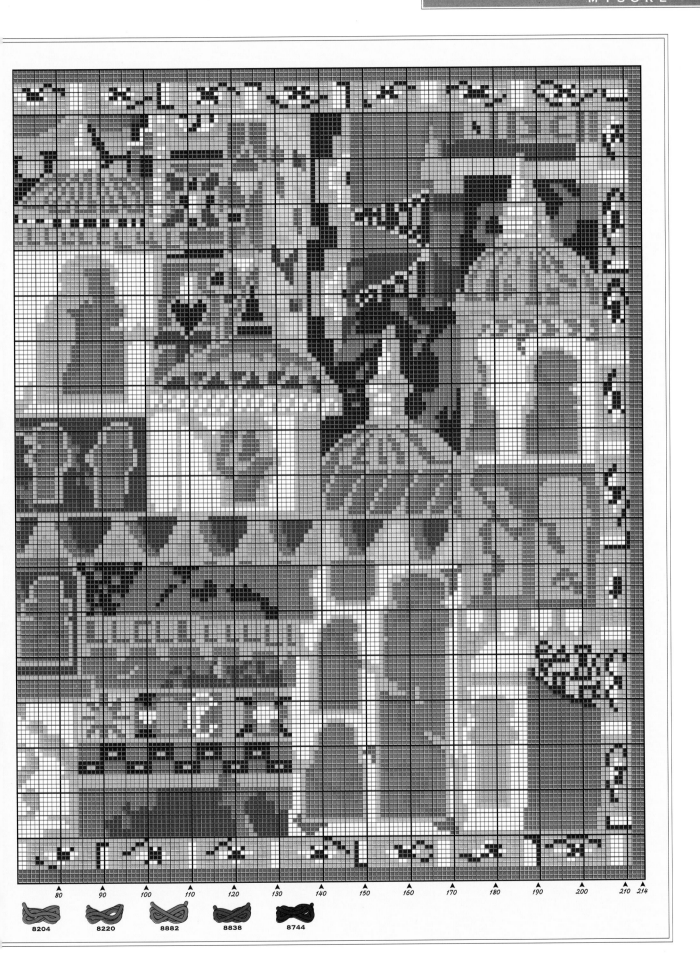

80 90 100 110 120 130 140 150 160 170 180 190 200 210 214

8204   8220   8882   8838   8744

JAIPUR STRIPE

We move on to Annabel Nellist's next Indian design, 'Jaipur Stripe'. Many of the colours are the same but there is the noticeable addition of green which alters the overall colour balance. Here Annabel uses thin strips of patchwork pattern vertically, whereas the patchwork skyline of 'Mysore' was constructed on the horizontal; and the association with eastern textiles is even more direct. The small areas of colour are interesting to work but not difficult. The blocks of colour may be small but they are clearly defined which avoids the complexity of gradual shading found in many of our other kits.

I am sure one of the reasons this design has proved so popular is that it is easy to live with. Interior design goes through its cycles like everything else and Indian design has been in the ascendant lately, but a pattern like 'Jaipur Stripe' is perennial. It looks comfortable in a wide variety of settings from the traditional and stately to the cleanest, most open of contemporary spaces. It could be argued that Persian and eastern carpets have generally proved to be one of the most enduring constants of European interiors. For six or seven hundred years these carpets have been found on the floors, or earlier on the tables, of European houses. Architectural styles and tastes in furniture have come and gone. Fashions in fabrics, paint colours and wallpapers have evolved, along with the scale and use of rooms, but the eastern carpet remains. And it remains, like a rock of ages, largely unaltered. The same carpet looks as happily at home on the table in a Holbein painting as it does on the floor of a 1990s New York apartment. You would not be surprised to find an eastern carpet in any home, old or new, and the same goes for Annabel Nellist's 'Jaipur Stripe'. Her use of pattern is different, her motifs and colours distinctive, but in essence this cushion cover remains in the tradition of eastern carpet design.

Annabel has dotted birds and architectural motifs over the pattern in a delightfully random manner. This is a common feature of Indian embroidery. Embroidered quilts called Kanthas are made throughout Bengal by all castes of women, both Hindu and Muslim. The patterns and figures – often birds and animals – have symbolic significance, as they did for Elizabethan embroiderers. Their placing and colouring is entirely a matter for the individual embroiderer. As a result no two Kanthas are alike and they are infused with the spontaneity so typical of folk art around the world. Annabel adopts this style with her birds all facing in different directions. Combined with her balanced but asymmetric use of pattern she has evoked a truly Indian flavour.

Another designer who has always appreciated that the vitality of eastern design lies in its irregularity is Kaffe Fassett. There are none of his carpet-inspired designs in this book but those of you who are familiar with his work will know what I mean. He always keeps his outlines rough to capture the authentic, human feel of handmade textiles. It often surprises me how few textile designers see the importance of this. So many of the kelim patterns around at the moment look dead. The reason is simple: they have neat, straight lines and regular repeats. Stitched geometric patterns come alive when things start to go wrong! Or, to put it more soberly, the eye is caught by a different outline or a dash of colour appearing unexpectedly. This personalises the design adding a new layer of depth to the pattern. Embroidery, being free-form and subject to no mechanical restrictions, allows for such an approach. That is why it has the potential for being the most creative of all the textile arts. It is an advantage which gives the stitcher far greater freedom of expression than the weaver, block printer or fabric designer.

ANNABEL NELLIST IS A TEXTILE DESIGNER BY TRAINING AND THIS
IS EVIDENT IN HER NEEDLEWORK. SHE HAS ALSO PRODUCED CARDS,
BOOKMARKS AND OTHER TYPES OF STATIONERY BUT HER STYLE IS
PARTICULARLY WELL SUITED TO FABRICS

Annabel has recently adapted this design for a rug and it works well. She uses a twelve mesh canvas here to capture the detail but you could enlarge this design by transferring it on to a ten mesh canvas. Many people prefer larger cushions and these eastern textile patterns are particularly suitable. If you used a ten mesh canvas the cushion would measure 21½in × 18in (54cm × 46cm) which is a comfortable size for sinking into. You need to be careful about using different canvas sizes. There is usually a good reason why a designer has chosen a particular gauge. Many designs would look crude if they were simply enlarged in this way, but there is enough detail in 'Jaipur Stripe' to justify it in this case. It is also a question of scale. The largest single motif or block of colour is probably the bird in the bottom right hand corner, which is not very big. With no particular section of pattern predominating an increase in the overall size of roughly twenty per cent will not look odd or alter the character of the design. Either way working from the chart gives you the chance to choose your own size.

CANVAS: 12 holes to the inch

STITCH: Half-cross or tent

DESIGN AREA: 18in × 15in (46cm × 36cm)

YARN: Paternayan

Shade	Paternayan	
Caramel	442	5 skeins
Honey Yellow	732	2 skeins
Honey Yellow	734	3 skeins
Grey	202	1 skein
Deep Blue	570	3 skeins
Peacock Green	520	4 skeins
Peacock Green	521	2 skeins
Pine Green	662	2 skeins
Cream	263	3 skeins
Fawn	444	3 skeins
Cherry Red	840	4 skeins
Old Rose	D211	3 skeins
Damson	920	4 skeins
Khaki	453	3 skeins

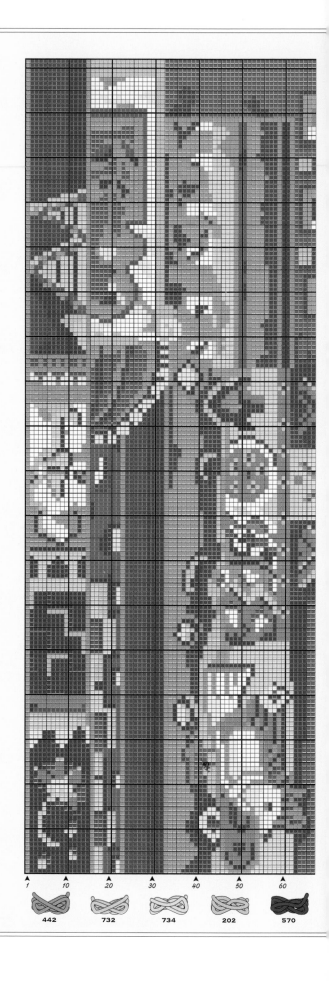

| 70 | 80 | 90 | 100 | 110 | 120 | 130 | 140 | 150 | 160 | 170 | 180 | 190 | 200 | 210 |

| 520 | 521 | 662 | 263 | 444 | 840 | D211 | 920 | 453 |

THE OWL

All of the designs in this first chapter have been inspired by, or are based on, textile patterns. But stylistically that is all that links this eclectic group. It illustrates the enormous breadth and variety of textile design around the world, and we now jump with dramatic contrast from India to England in the 1880s and the work of William Morris.

William Morris has to be the best known and best loved British textile designer of that century. In recent years we have seen rather too many Morris-style pastiches gracing everything from tea-towels and tapestry kits to t-shirts and mugs. Yet despite this unrelenting saturation the appeal of his work remains as strong as ever. In 1980 Ehrman produced a kit in association with the Royal School of Needlework called 'Victorian Bird'. We incorrectly ascribed it to William Morris. This stirred up a hornet's nest generating a furious correspondence from Morris fans pointing out our error. It also sold like hot cakes. It was a reasonable enough design but there was no doubt that the magic name of William Morris acted as a talisman for needleworkers. This episode opened my eyes to the extent of Morris's following. His appeal endures because he produced so much of quality, and there is still work of his to be rediscovered. When Neil McCallum showed me his painted canvas of the 'Owl' I was amazed that I had not seen this particular design before.

This design is based on one of Morris's woven tapestries which were heavily influenced by Flemish Verdure pieces. Perhaps the best known of this group was the 'Woodpecker' produced in 1885. William Morris's most successful tapestry designs were collaborations with Burne-Jones. But an overlooked contribution, and an important one, was made by John Henry Dearle. Dearle had started as an assistant at the Oxford Street shop but soon developed his own strong ideas on design. He designed many of the backgrounds for Morris's tapestries and was responsible for the familiar flowing floral patterns which he adapted from seventeenth-century Italian silks.

Neil McCallum has quite rightly used a fine mesh of canvas for this hanging. It does, however, use a lot of wool. This panel is a very practical shape; there are few homes which would have difficulty finding a place for it. Neil is now working on its companion for our next catalogue.

CANVAS: 13 holes to the inch

STITCH: Half-cross or tent

DESIGN AREA: 32in × 19½in (82cm × 49cm)

YARN: Appleton Tapestry wool or Paternayan

Shade	Appleton	Paternayan	
Iron Grey	965	200	2 skeins
Honeysuckle Yellow	692	754	8 skeins
Honeysuckle Yellow	695	732	9 skeins
Autumn Yellow	476	722	5 skeins
Sea Green	407	660	49 skeins
Rose Pink	759	900	3 skeins
Kingfisher	488	580	3 skeins
Sky Blue	564	584	3 skeins
Sky Blue	562	555	2 skeins
Grass Green	254	692	2 skeins
Early English Green	542	653	3 skeins
Purple	105	311	1 skein
Rose Pink	755	D275	5 skeins
Olive Green	243	642	4 skeins
Golden Brown	903	442	2 skeins
Dull Rose Pink	146	910	2 skeins
Bright Rose Pink	941	934	3 skeins
Purple	103	312	2 skeins
Pastel Lilac	885	313	1 skein
Red Fawn	305	400	1 skein
Autumn Yellow	478	721	1 skein
Chocolate	183	453	2 skeins
Chocolate	184	432	2 skeins
Turquoise	524	D502	2 skeins
Turquoise	526	D501	2 skeins

HENRY DEARLE WORKED FOR WILLIAM MORRIS BUT THIS WAS
VERY MUCH HIS OWN DESIGN. IT WAS WORKED IN SILKS ON A
WOVEN SILK DAMASK GROUND AROUND 1890

965

692

695

476

407

759

488

564

562

254

542

105

755

243 903 146 941 103 885 305 478 183 184 524 526

MAYTIME

It is most appropriate that we should retrace our steps from William Morris to the world of medieval tapestry. In Morris's opinion the medieval and Gothic period, up to about 1500, represented the high watermark for tapestry design. From the fourteenth century tapestry was clearly seen as one of the major decorative arts. Despite the decline in church hangings (larger windows and more space for tombs) the workshops of Brussels, Arras and Tournai were fully occupied providing made-to-measure hangings for castles, palaces and large homes throughout Europe. It is a period that has fascinated Candace Bahouth for years and, in terms of needlework design, she has made it her own.

Candace's book *Medieval Needlepoint* (1993) was a pageant of richly patterned ornament, symbol and emblem. Lions, unicorns, fleur-de-lys, heraldry and the constellations crowd the pages. Her colours epitomise the period – dense and sumptuous burgundies, royal blue, raspberry pink and gold. The woven hangings from which she takes her inspiration rejoice in the regenerative magic of nature, their backgrounds filled with field upon field of individual flowers. The example that springs most immediately to mind is the series of the 'Lady with Unicorn' in the Cluny Museum in Paris and it was this series which inspired Candace's 'Rug of Flowers' which can be seen pictured with Maytime on pages 26 and 27.

Candace's millefleurs patterns faithfully reproduce the sinuous, elongated elegance of medieval embroidered flowers. Lesser copies are always too squat. She then arranges them to form a balanced picture while taking equal care to balance her colours. To maintain the movement and informality of the design the odd leaf overlaps the border. Her borders have a very personal stamp to them and this one is no exception. The four sides are all different – no mirror

CANDACE BAHOUTH HAS MADE A NAME FOR HERSELF
WITH HER MEDIEVAL DESIGNS. HER KNOWLEDGE AND LOVE
OF THE PERIOD IS SELF-EVIDENT

images here – and although motifs recur, their spacing and coalition varies from side to side. This in turn adds to the rug's vitality in a subtle yet essential way. Many other designers would have structured this border more formally and would have lost much of the rug's liveliness as a result. Her simple, effective use of colour, combining burgundy and gold, shows what restrained good taste is all about and, to my eye, the scale and balance of this composition could not be improved upon.

'Maytime', with its similar border, colouring and floral theme was designed to go with the 'Rug of Flowers'. It is a lovely cushion in its own right and has proved one of Candace's most popular.

Candace's borders are wonderful. It would be possible to use this one to make a photograph or mirror frame. We have never produced kits for frames as everyone wants a different size, but a chart allows you to adapt the pattern yourself. Kaffe Fassett had a lovely lichen-patterned frame in *Glorious Needlepoint* and Mary Norden had a number in her last book *Mary Norden's Needlepoint*. This chart also illustrates Candace's skill with backgrounds. She rarely uses a single flat colour. By mixing two close, complementary colours she recreates the faded, weathered look of older textiles. For those of you who stitch your own designs here is a good example of how to achieve this effect with relative simplicity. But make sure when you mix your two sets of colour that you do so randomly, otherwise you could produce a regular pattern.

CANVAS: 10 holes to the inch

STITCH: Half-cross or tent

DESIGN AREA: 16in × 16in (41cm × 41cm)

YARN: Appleton Tapestry wool or Paternayan

Shade	Appleton	Paternayan	
Dull Rose Pink	142	923	1 skein
Mid Blue	157	531	6 skeins
Mid Blue	158	531	6 skeins
Flame Red	209	D211	6 skeins
Bright Terracotta	225	931	4 skeins
Jacobean Green	292	603	2 skeins
Sea Green	401	613	3 skeins
Autumn Yellow	472	703	1 skein
Honeysuckle Yellow	694	733	4 skeins
Bright China Blue	743	561	1 skein
Rose Pink	755	D275	1 skein
Royal Blue	821	543	1 skein
Heraldic Gold	841	704	1 skein
Custard Yellow	851	D541	1 skein
Pastel Cream	882	263	1 skein
Golden Brown	903	442	6 skeins
Bright Rose Pink	947	902	1 skein
Drab Fawn	954	453	1 skein
Rust	994	852	1 skein

| 142 | 158 | 225 | 401 | 694 | 755 | 851 | 882 | 947 | 994 |

| 157 | 209 | 292 | 472 | 743 | 821 | 841 | 903 | 954 |

OVERLEAF: THE RUG OF FLOWERS PROVIDED

THE INSPIRATION AND MATERIAL FOR A PAIR OF

MATCHING CUSHIONS OF WHICH MAYTIME HAS

PROVED THE MOST POPULAR

BERLIN ROSES

We end this chapter with a look at Berlin Woolwork patterns of the 1860s. Here is a design based squarely and unashamedly on the stitched textiles of that time and the actual pattern charts of the day formed the basis of the design.

Three years ago we were approached by Sotheby who had a miscellaneous collection of Berlin Woolwork charts in one of their forthcoming sales. They wondered if we would be interested in buying them by private treaty in advance of the auction. I was intrigued and went along to have a look. On the whole these high Victorian charted patterns are not really our scene. They tend to consist of pastoral landscapes – shepherds set in bucolic idylls – children with pets, tight little compositions of birds and fruits and suffocating excesses with cabbage roses. However, looking at this very mixed bag of charted patterns, one feature stood out: whoever put them together knew how to draw. These charts have a static, three-dimensional stillness to them. The stereoscopic clarity is achieved by using a very fine graph paper (twenty-four squares to the inch or finer), lots of colours for shading and a rigorous application of scientific proportion when dealing with leaves and flowers. The effect is eerie but rather fascinating. It struck me that we could extract different sections and recreate our own patterns using existing elements from within the designs. David Merry, who has great experience at producing needlework charts, was the obvious choice for the job and he set about his task with relish. He chopped and changed, amalgamated and repositioned till the 'Berlin Roses' emerged – a hybrid construct of contemporary and 1860s design. We then stitched them in paler, fresher colours to maintain this more contemporary feel and I think they have turned out very well.

The charts themselves used, on average, over thirty colours. The maximum number of colours we can print is around twenty-five, so another of David's jobs was to simplify the colours without losing the detailed shading of the originals. Here again he has done an excellent job.

This style of needlework became known as Berlin Woolwork because the early charts were produced by two Berlin print-sellers, Mme Wittich and Herr Philipson, who commissioned embroidery designs for reproduction on graph paper. They became popular for two main reasons. Groups of women could stitch and chat at the same time making needlework a more social activity, and by the technical

needlework standards of the day they were relatively easy. In a way they were the precursors of the printed kits of today and they sold in large numbers. After the success of 'Berlin Roses' we were bitten by the bug and are now producing a series along the same lines. The second one that David designed for us can be seen in the final chapter.

IN NEEDLEWORK, IT SEEMS, THE ROSE SHALL NEITHER WITHER NOR FADE. IT IS A PERENNIAL, REDISCOVERED BY SUCCEEDING GENERATIONS OF STITCHERS

1 10 20 30 40 50 60 70 80 90 100 110 120 130

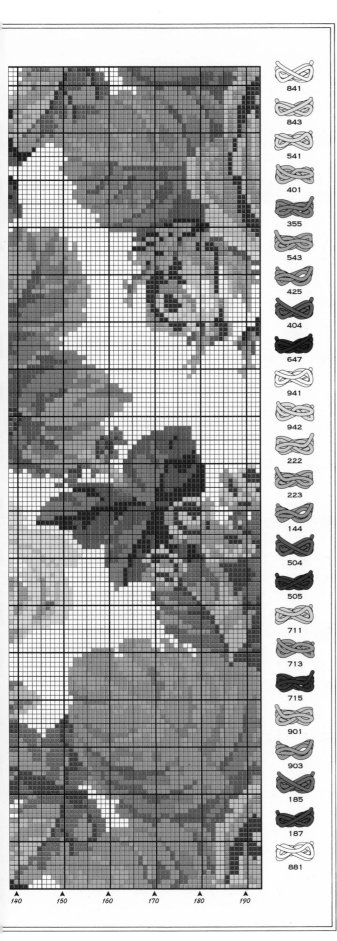

This design is ideal for choosing your own background colour. We have suggested a couple of options. Another idea for background colouring is to use two contrasting tones and to use them in different sections of the background. Looking at the design there are basically five areas of background colour that are stitched in blocks. Try alternating each of these blocks in cream or charcoal grey. It sounds alarming but looks very stylish. Or, to achieve an antique look, stitch the background area mixing two tones of your chosen colour. Stitching in this speckled, random manner will give a much richer, textural quality to the pattern.

CANVAS: 12 holes to the inch

STITCH: Half-cross or tent

DESIGN AREA: 14in × 15in (36cm × 38cm)

YARN: Appleton Tapestry wool or Paternayan

Shade	Appleton	Paternayan	
Heraldic Gold	841	704	5 skeins
Heraldic Gold	843	733	1 skein
Early English Green	541	644	1 skein
Sea Green	401	613	1 skein
Grey Green	355	603	4 skeins
Early English Green	543	693	3 skeins
Leaf Green	425	621	3 skeins
Sea Green	404	611	3 skeins
Peacock Blue	647	660	2 skeins
Bright Rose Pink	941	934	1 skein
Bright Rose Pink	942	933	1 skein
Bright Terracotta	222	933	2 skeins
Bright Terracotta	223	D275	1 skein
Dull Rose Pink	144	912	1 skein
Scarlet	504	950	1 skein
Scarlet	505	940	2 skeins
Wine Red	711	914	1 skein
Wine Red	713	912	1 skein
Wine Red	715	910	1 skein
Golden Brown	901	443	2 skeins
Golden Brown	903	442	2 skeins
Chocolate	185	431	2 skeins
Chocolate	187	430	2 skeins

Background (choose one colour)

Pastel Cream	881	262	1 hank
Scarlet	504	950	1 hank

31

TEXTILES

Chapter Two

~

THE
SEA

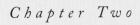 "Of all the objects I have seen,
there is none which affects my
imagination so much as the sea or ocean.
I cannot see the heaving of this prodigious
bulk of water, even in a calm, without a
pleasing astonishment."

JOSEPH ADDISON'S
ESSAY ON THE SEA IN THE *SPECTATOR*, 1712

ROMAN MOSAIC

The 'leisure age' envisaged in the 1960s never quite happened. One of the misalignments of the modern world is the division of labour. It is an accepted paradox that those in work (in the West) are working harder than ever, with increasingly long hours, while the number of those with no work at all stays stubbornly high. In the sunlit uplands of the computer age work was meant to be spread around in ever decreasing quantities. With technology able to do so many human tasks we would, in theory, have shorter, more flexible working hours. With the increased productivity and efficiency that technology brings greater wealth would be generated creating higher living standards. The combination of higher living standards and more free time would result in a blossoming of artistic activity as we would all have the time and money to pursue our creative interests. Well that was the theory! Not many of us would recognise it as the reality of today. Yet, curiously enough, it still remains a remote prospect for the next century if we can somehow learn to arrange our new world of work more intelligently.

In conjunction with the advance of computer technology other major sociological changes are taking place. Part-time working is becoming far more widespread, we are retiring earlier and we are living longer. So despite longer hours for some there is more spare time for others. The huge growth in interest in gardening, cooking, travel and indeed craftwork testifies to this. There is more disposable wealth in total than ever before (even if it doesn't feel like it!) and time has been liberated not only by different working practices but by labour-saving domestic appliances. These changes, gathering pace and affecting the balance in our lives between work and leisure, should indicate that needlework is a craft of the future.

Ten or twenty years ago needlework was perceived as a genteel, fading pastime which by the turn of the century would be virtually extinct. But as the years have gone by our customers have become younger. It is not only a question of design, it is also the nature of the craft. It is exactly the sort of activity suited to a future world of fragmented work where those with time look for some form of artistic fulfilment. So long as the visual content remains innovative and exciting needlework should appeal to a new generation of stitchers. It is a relaxing way to unwind and many of our younger customers comment on the therapeutic nature of stitching our kits. Needlework is not a fashion industry but it does need to move along with the times. This chapter reflects that approach and I think you will find that nearly all the designs here have a fresher, cleaner, more contemporary feel to them.

As an island nation we have always had a fascination with the sea. How odd then that aquatic images feature so rarely in needlework design. Might this have something to do with the nature of the sea? The boundless deep has a mesmeric quality but it is dangerous. All maritime peoples have a healthy respect for the sea. The great descriptions of storm and tempest in the writings of Conrad, Dickens, Byron or Tennyson are descriptions of primeval force beyond human control. The reassuring images of pastoral life or historical allegory have, in the past, been psychologically better suited to a sedate and domestic pastime like needlework. Maybe I am quite wrong about this, it is only an idea, but I find it interesting that according to Christie's views of calm waters always sell best in their maritime art sales. In any event the sea affords a wealth of decorative possibilities for the stitcher, most of them largely unexplored. Shells appear in needlework but fish, amphibians, ships or waves hardly ever.

Helen Townley saw a picture of a Roman tile in a Christie's catalogue and was inspired to turn it into a tapestry. Her colours are soft and catch the movement and shading of her subject. Most fish slither by in subdued blends of neutrals – or at least they do in the cooler waters familiar to the Roman world – and, rather surprisingly, that is why she needed so many colours for such a 'colourless' design. This particular tile needed little adaptation to become a cushion cover. When Helen saw it she felt the shape, composition and scale were perfect unaltered and her skill has been in transcribing the original ceramic colours into needlework.

HELEN TOWNLEY'S ROMAN TILE PATTERN CAME TO US

UNSOLICITED THROUGH THE POST. IT IS VERY RARE FOR SUCH

QUALITY TO ARRIVE IN THIS WAY AND, TAKING ADVANTAGE OF OUR

WINDFALL, WE PUT IT STRAIGHT INTO PRODUCTION

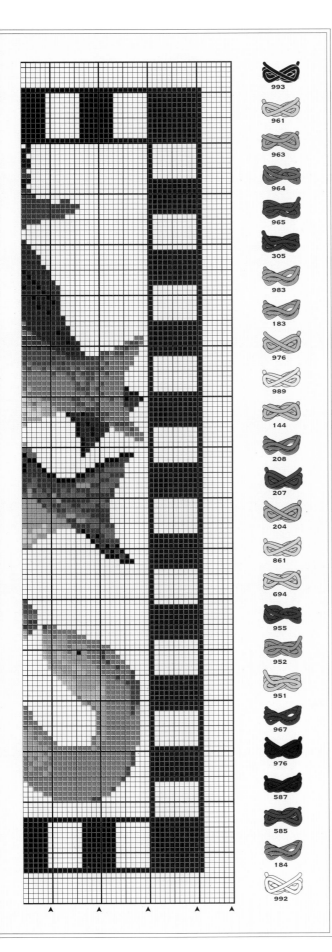

Personally I'm not mad about the border; I find it a bit heavy. You could leave it out completely, or stitch a simpler geometric border on a smaller scale; or in softer colours. An alternative background could be black, or even a deep sea blue would provide enough contrast. This is a good chart to use as a design source.

CANVAS: 10 holes to the inch

STITCH: Half-cross or tent

DESIGN AREA: 16in × 16in (41cm × 41cm)

YARN: Appleton Tapestry wool or Paternayan

Shade	Appleton	Paternayan	
Black	993	220	6 skeins
Iron Grey	961	204	1 skein
Iron Grey	963	202	1 skein
Iron Grey	964	201	1 skein
Iron Grey	965	200	1 skein
Red Fawn	305	400	1 skein
Putty Grounding	983	463	1 skein
Putty Grounding	989	246	1 skein
Dull Rose Pink	144	912	1 skein
Flame Red	207	870	2 skeins
Flame Red	208	870	1 skein
Flame Red	204	485	1 skein
Coral	861	855	1 skein
Honeysuckle Yellow	694	733	1 skein
Drab Fawn	955	452	1 skein
Drab Fawn	952	453	1 skein
Drab Fawn	951	454	1 skein
Iron Grey	967	200	2 skeins
Elephant Grey	976	461	1 skein
Brown Grounding	587	421	1 skein
Brown Grounding	585	421	1 skein
White	992	263	17 skeins
Chocolate	184	432	1 skein
Chocolate	183	453	1 skein

NOTE: This chart design differs very slightly from that available in kit form.

THE SEA

CRAB AND LOBSTER

The geometric backdrops to Kaffe Fassett's 'Crab' and 'Lobster' are bold and dramatic and illustrative of his 'gutsy' approach to design at its best. He loves to experiment not only with new colour combinations but also with new subjects for needlework. It comes as no surprise that he should have chosen lobsters and crabs. These two splendid creatures were originally stitched together as a pair for a shoulder bag in his book *Glorious Needlepoint*. The chequerboard background of the bag, reminiscent of fishmongers tiles, was suggested by Steve Lovi,

the photographer. For these two cushions Kaffe has added touches of mustard, brown and lilac to soften the harsh black and white of the backdrop and it gives it a new depth. These off colours have an almost 1950s flavour to them. On the other hand, if you prefer the crisp clarity of black and white the chart allows you to stitch them in this way. Kaffe's shading of both the lobster and the crab is superb and it is a shining example of how effectively a good artist can work with a limited number of wools. Looking at them you would think that at least twenty colours were used in each. Kaffe purposely restricted himself to around ten per crustacean to keep the cost of the kits down. No other needlework designer could have shaded as subtly with so few colours; and no other needlework designer could have stitched these shells with such precision.

I HAD ALWAYS ADMIRED THE CRAB AND LOBSTER ON KAFFE FASSETT'S SHOULDER BAG IN *GLORIOUS NEEDLEPOINT* AND, AFTER SO MANY YEARS, I SUGGESTED WE SHOULD LOOK AT THEM AGAIN. THE RESULT IS THIS IMAGINATIVE PAIR OF CUSHIONS. BOTH THE 'LOBSTER' AND THE 'CRAB' ILLUSTRATE KAFFE'S INIMITABLE SKILL AT SHADING. THESE ARE THE WORKS OF A TRUE ARTIST

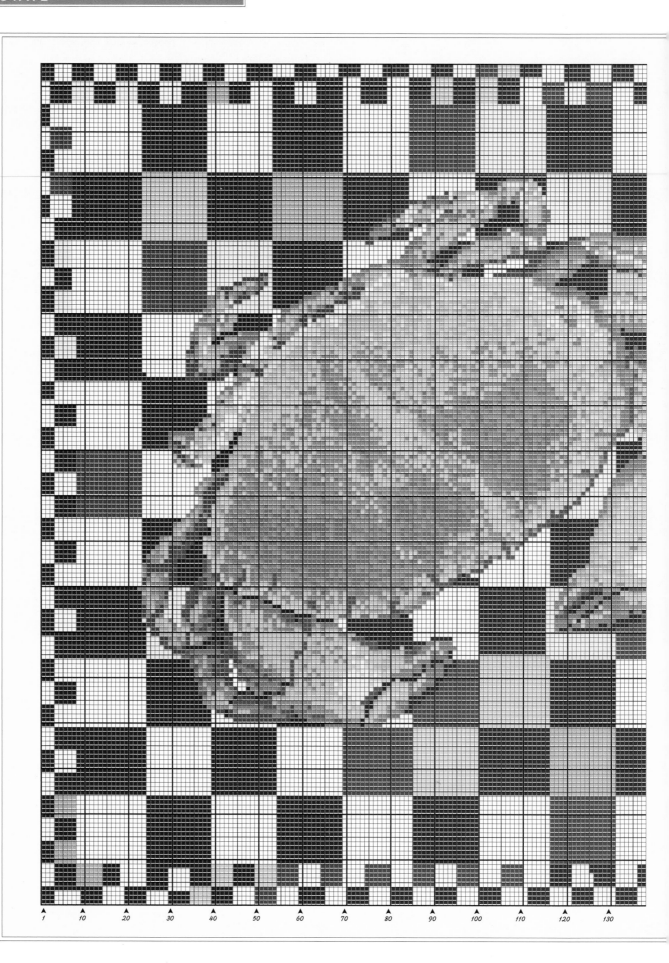

1   10   20   30   40   50   60   70   80   90   100   110   120   130

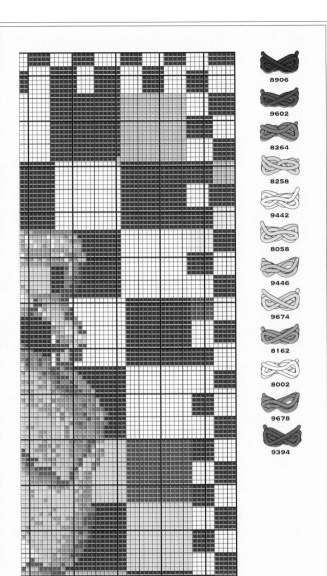

8906	
9602	
8264	
8258	
9442	
8058	
9446	
9674	
8162	
8002	
9678	
9394	

140 150 160 170 180 187

Both the crab and the lobster would look wonderful on plain coloured backgrounds. I would love to see them stitched on black. Their warm colours and the delicacy of Kaffe's shading would shine out from a deep, neutral background. They would look as striking as his individual fruits series did when stitched on bottle green. If they were on a single-coloured background they could even be used for chairseats (how about sitting on a crab?). They could be stitched together in alternate squares to make a rug or you could revert to Kaffe's original idea by using them for a shoulder bag – one on each side. Or just take one and use it repeatedly: a rug of crabs all crawling in different directions could be interesting. These are just a few ideas for what you could do with these dramatic images.

CANVAS: 10 holes to the inch

STITCH: Half-cross or tent

DESIGN AREA: $17\frac{1}{2}$in × 18in (44cm × 46cm)

YARN: Anchor Tapisserie or Paternayan

Shade	Anchor	Paternayan	
Sea Green	8906	660	9 skeins
Mahogany	9602	860	3 skeins
Terracotta	8264	861	2 skeins
Terracotta	8258	863	3 skeins
Nutmeg	9442	886	2 skeins
Autumn Gold	8058	804	1 skein
Nutmeg	9446	413	3 skeins
Mink	9674	D133	2 skeins
Rust Orange	8162	851	3 skeins
White	8002	261	7 skeins
Mink	9678	D123	2 skeins
Cinnamon	9394	440	1 skein

These cushions show how clever Kaffe is with simple geo-metric borders. The two thin strips of smaller squares have a soft, speckled feel, like confetti. It is a very simple way to soften the geometric regularity of the main background, and by echoing the central colours (but in an irregular man-ner) he softens the design still further. Most borders enclose, this one drifts pattern outwards. By doing so it focuses the eye firmly on the lobster and adds to the three-dimensional quality of the design. The cushion looks as though it is spilling over the edge with the lobster walking on top. It is a small touch but it is integral to the design's success.

CANVAS: 10 holes to the inch

STITCH: Half-cross or tent

DESIGN AREA: 18in × 18in (46cm × 46cm)

YARN: Anchor Tapisserie or Paternayan

Shade	Anchor	Paternayan	
Mahogany	9602	860	3 skeins
Sea Green	8906	660	13 skeins
Terracotta	8264	861	2 skeins
Cinnamon	9382	465	6 skeins
Paprika	8234	862	3 skeins
Rust Orange	8162	851	4 skeins
Sand	9524	803	2 skeins
Flame Red	8196	821	4 skeins
Salmon Pink	8306	864	2 skeins
White	8002	261	8 skeins
Oak Brown	9402	445	1 skein

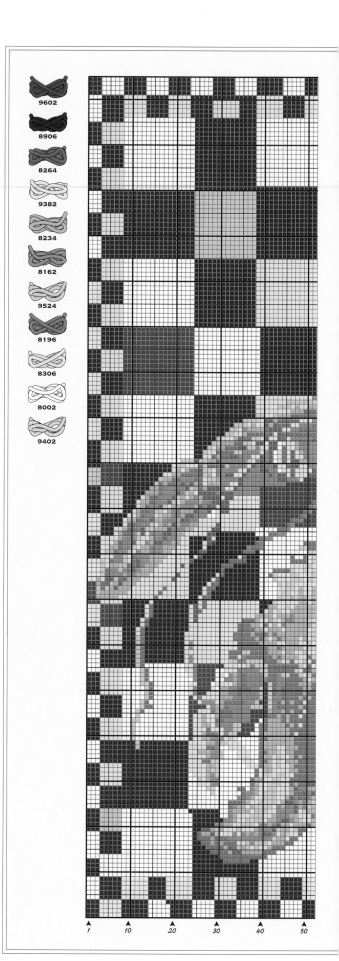

SHELLS
WAISTCOAT

I think there can be very little doubt that Kaffe Fassett is the most varied and interesting needlework designer of our times. The colour blends in some of his knitting are wonderful, his wallpapers are distinctive and his new rag rugs look interesting. I personally think that some of the fabric designs for Designers' Guild are amongst his best work, but it is in his needlework that so many skills come together: his draughtsmanship and natural facility at drawing, his unique colour sense and his use of wool as the chosen medium for his own brand of painting. To have said this four or five years ago would have been extravagant, especially as the focus was then on his knitting. The body of work which he has now produced makes such a claim more credible. No one else has produced such a range of design in this field since William Morris – certainly not in this country. I really can think of no one from the intervening years who could make such a claim. You may love his work or you may hate it but his significance as a textile designer is indisputable.

He is the only living needlework designer with a truly international following. When 107,000 people pay to see an exhibition of his work in Stockholm it is clear that this international following is substantial. The scope and scale of his work is unparalleled. In the sixteen years we have worked with him he has produced nearly 150 cushion covers, ten large carpets, rugs and hanging panels, and numerous smaller spectacle case, slipper, shoulder-bag and chairseat kits. He stitches these himself with the help of one or two trusted assistants. During that same period he has produced

KAFFE FASSETT, WHO DESIGNED THE FIRST
EHRMAN NEEDLEPOINT KIT, IS STILL THE PRINCIPAL DESIGNER,
CONTRIBUTING OVER TEN NEW DESIGNS TO THE
EHRMAN RANGE EVERY YEAR

over fifty highly detailed commissioned pieces, using as many as a hundred colours in each, ranging from large pieces of furniture to delicately stitched waistcoats. And all of this while simultaneously designing knitwear for Rowan, ranges of wallpapers and fabrics for Designers' Guild, writing seven books, appearing in his own television series, touring the world opening exhibitions, giving lectures and workshops, and generally promoting all of these activities. He is one of the very few workaholics I have met in my life. 'Workaholic' is a much misused term. It is quite different from a very hard worker. A workaholic observes no restrictions on working hours whatsoever; it is a total obsession, an all consuming passion. Kaffe is one of that very rare breed. He will sometimes stitch right through the night and always works on trains or aeroplanes as he can't bear to waste any time when travelling. Driven by his creative demons it is as though one lifetime were not enough for all he has to do.

With such a prodigious output, produced at such torrential speed, quality will inevitably vary. Some artists – Picasso, Rowlandson or Pugin being obvious, august examples – work at this explosive pace and are unconcerned with self-editing; while others refine and perfect, more conscious of the critical gaze of history. These are grand examples but they illustrate a general split among artists, at all levels of ability, in how they approach their work. Kaffe is firmly in the former tradition and is interested in everything that he produces. His work is like a diary. However, looking at the body of his work as a whole, I am astonished how few duds there have been. Although his work is often experimental, his standards are high and the rare Kaffe Fassett 'dud' would stand comparison with the better efforts of many lesser designers. At some point in the future a retrospective exhibition of his work will be mounted, edited down to the really good examples of his various styles, and it will show

that he is without question the foremost needlework designer of our age.

I spoke of the range of his design. He has a voracious appetite for novel source material and is usually the first with a new theme: Eastern textiles, vegetables, fruits, faces, farmyard animals, fans and shells were all originally his ideas for commercial needlepoint kits. Nearly all of these themes have been subsequently taken-up by other needlepoint kit companies. This has never worried Kaffe as he hates to repeat himself and is always moving on to the next subject. It is part of his generous nature that he has always regarded imitation as flattery. Few would deny that in this field he sets the pace. In any case nearly all these subjects have appeared in older tapestries or embroideries anyway. The fact is that Kaffe is just more imaginative in his plundering of the past than his more timid imitators. And once he gets an idea it becomes his own, a good example of this being his series of stitched shells.

Over the past few years Kaffe has stitched a shell and turtle rug, a shells cushion and his waistcoat, seen here. All of these are featured in his own book published in autumn 1995. I am most grateful to him for allowing me to include the waistcoat in this book as well. I felt that no chapter on the sea would be complete without at least one example of his shell patterns and it is particularly nice to have a waistcoat for a change. The kit comes with two canvases, for the left and right hand side, printed for one size only. To change the fit you need to vary the width of material at the back to suit your size. It works well and the only thing to look out for is whether or not the overall length of the waistcoat will be correct. The waistcoat is edged with piping to provide the buttonholes. I love the way the shells blend into the sand and you need to stand back to see their outlines clearly emerge. Shells slippers are following next which should be fun.

THE FIRST WAISTCOAT KIT WE PRODUCED. SOME OF KAFFE'S COMMISSIONED WAISTCOATS ARE BREATHTAKING AND A SERIES OF THEM WERE RECENTLY PHOTOGRAPHED FOR GREETINGS CARDS. THEY ARE AMONGST HIS FINEST NEEDLEPOINT DESIGNS

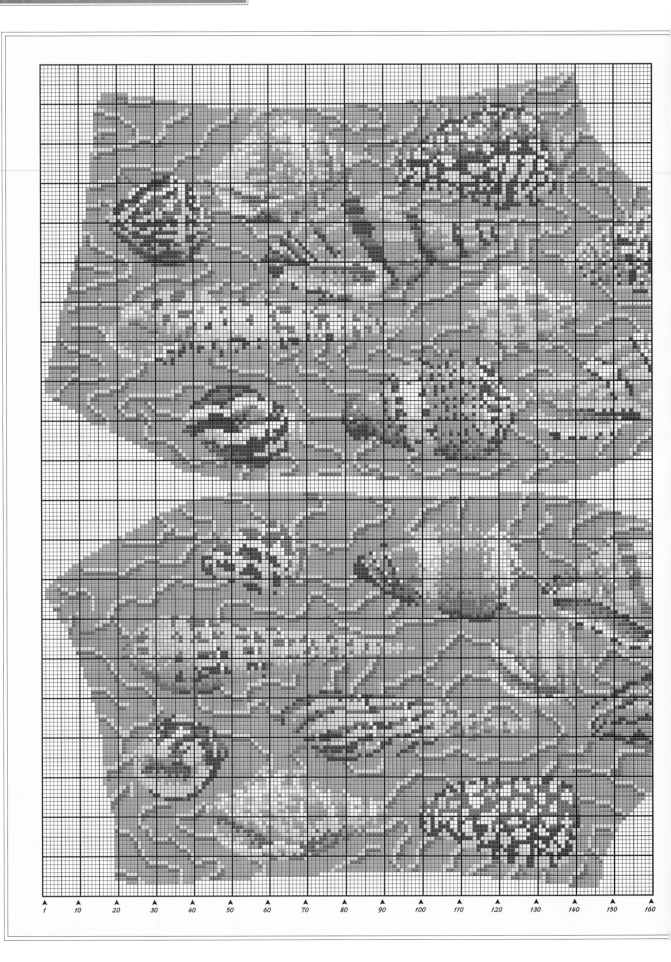

1   10   20   30   40   50   60   70   80   90   100   110   120   130   140   150   160

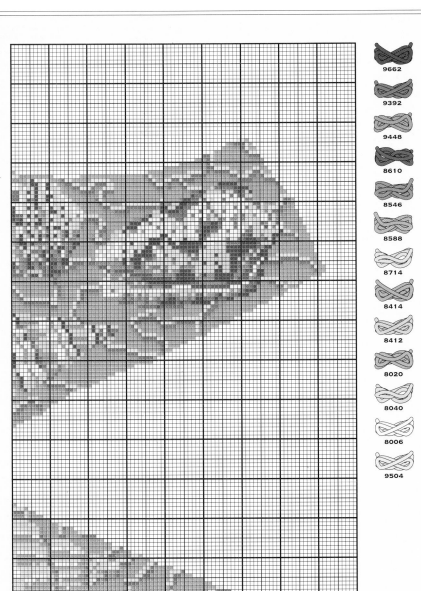

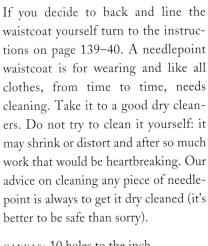

9662		
9392		
9448		
8610		
8546		
8588		
8714		
8414		
8412		
8020		
8040		
8006		
9504		

If you decide to back and line the waistcoat yourself turn to the instructions on page 139–40. A needlepoint waistcoat is for wearing and like all clothes, from time to time, needs cleaning. Take it to a good dry cleaners. Do not try to clean it yourself: it may shrink or distort and after so much work that would be heartbreaking. Our advice on cleaning any piece of needlepoint is always to get it dry cleaned (it's better to be safe than sorry).

CANVAS: 10 holes to the inch

STITCH: Half-cross or tent

DESIGN AREA: Top of neck to bottom of front points is 24in (61cm). Underarm to waist is 12in (30cm). Each front measures 10in (25cm) across. When backed it can be altered in size to fit up to 40in (102cm) bust.

YARN: Anchor Tapisserie or Paternayan

Shade	Anchor	Paternayan	
Chocolate	9662	460	5 skeins
Cinnamon	9392	441	8 skeins
Nutmeg	9448	403	7 skeins
Periwinkle	8610	341	2 skeins
Lavender	8546	323	1 skein
Lilac	8588	313	2 skeins
Steel Grey	8714	D392	3 skeins
Raspberry	8414	D281	2 skeins
Raspberry	8412	924	2 skeins
Old Gold	8020	733	15 skeins
Maize	8040	753	3 skeins
Cream	8006	263	4 skeins
Bronze Flesh	9504	493	8 skeins

49

THE SEA

170 180 190 200 210 220 230 240 250

BIRD CATCHING A FISH

Neil McCallum's 'Bird Catching a Fish' is based directly on a tile by William De Morgan and he manages to catch all the fluid movement found in the original. He also faithfully reproduces the fresh, clean colours of De Morgan's ceramic tile, colours which De Morgan developed himself. There has been a resurgence of interest in De Morgan's work – Beth Russell of Designers' Forum, for example, has used some of his tile patterns for her own needlepoint kits. It is easy to see why. As well as being a talented man with a distinctive signature he was an interesting one. We remember him as an artist-potter, but he was better known to contemporaries as the author of a series of novels all written between the age of sixty-seven and seventy-eight! A sort of Mary Wesley of his day. Looking at his ceramics now we can recognise in his approach a bridge between the mid-Victorian and the pre-Raphaelite world of William Morris. As a potter he is remembered best for his Persian styles, fabulous beasts (sometimes rather sinister combinations of animals), sailing ships and exotic floral designs. The floral designs are usually set against complex patterns of twining, twisting vegetation, and here is probably the closest link with the textiles of William Morris. He was fascinated by all things scientific and was continually experimenting with ceramic technique. His colours became more vivid as he grew older with the soft, glazed Persian colours of the early period at Chelsea giving way to lustre and iridescence in the late 1880s.

The tile which Neil McCallum has chosen is from De Morgan's Persian period and is one of the most successful of his designs in terms of composition and line. The bird is also one of the more pleasing of his fantastical creations – a combination of heron, stork and peacock by the look of it. Lewis Carroll was inspired to write *The Hunting of the Snark* by De Morgan tiles in his room at Oxford. The Jabberwock has its equivalent in De Morgan's dragons. The colours in the tile, dating from the early 1870s, used what he termed his Persian colours, a unique palette he developed consisting mainly of blue, turquoise, green and clear red. To capture the detail of the design, and more importantly to capture the clean sweep of De Morgan's lines, Neil McCallum has chosen a fourteen mesh canvas. Often a simple design requires a clear outline and the fourteen mesh canvas is an integral part of this design's success. We should not forget that this picture was painted onto a tile. It is Neil's ability to elaborate and alter that has enabled him to adapt the design just enough to translate into needlework without jeopardising the integrity of the original.

By the turn of the century taste and fashion were moving in a different direction. The influence of Japanese simplicity, a primitive rough quality to form and surface, and natural colour were themes that interested artist-potters. 'All my life I have been trying to make beautiful things and now that I can make them nobody wants them' said De Morgan sadly towards the end of his life. A similar fate befell William Morris and the whole of the Arts and Crafts movement. The seismic upheavals of modernism and the advent of the twentieth century swept them aside. Within a matter of years their work looked dated and quaintly irrelevant. It was light years away from Expressionist painting, the architectural theories of Le Corbusier or the pottery of Bernard Leach. Only now that the tide of this turbulent storm-sea is receding with an exhausted, querulous clamour can we glimpse again the quieter achievements of these late Victorian artists. Their aims were more modest but their achievements were real. Looking now at De Morgan's work for what it is, not for what it represented, we see the expression of a confident draughtsman with a pure, clear sense of colour, an imaginative mind and an idiosyncratic style.

NEIL MCCALLUM'S RENDERING OF A
WILLIAM DE MORGAN TILE DESIGN. AN EXPERT
ADAPTATION IN EVERY RESPECT

De Morgan's tiles excite us still today. It is not only their fantastic animal creations that make them unique, it is his bold, dramatic sense of design which fills the available surface with rhythmic patterns. The purity of his colours – blues, turquoise and greens in particular – add to this sense of authority. He was greatly influenced by Persian 'Isnik' tiles of the fifteenth and sixteenth centuries with their fluent swirls and exotic curves. His tiles are an excellent design source as many of them are complete pictures in themselves. I particularly like some of his ships. The Victoria and Albert Museum have published a selection of his tile designs and J. Catleugh's *William De Morgan (1839–1917) Tilemaker* was published in 1983. He designed the tile panels for the Tsar Alexander III's yacht *Livadia* and he filled the gaps in Lord Leighton's famous Arabian Hall at his Kensington house with copies of the genuine 'Isnik' tiles.

CANVAS: 14 holes to the inch

STITCH: Half-cross or tent

DESIGN AREA: 15in × 15in (38cm × 38cm)

YARN: Appleton Tapestry wool or Paternayan

Shade	Appleton	Paternayan	
Kingfisher	481	584	4 skeins
Kingfisher	484	591	2 skeins
Kingfisher	487	581	3 skeins
Signal Green	437	681	1 skein
Charcoal	998	221	2 skeins
Pastel Cream	882	263	9 skeins
Autumn Yellow	478	721	1 skein
Royal Blue	824	540	2 skeins
Autumn Yellow	475	723	2 skeins
Honeysuckle Yellow	693	734	1 skein
Bright Peacock Blue	831	D522	2 skeins
Bright Peacock Blue	833	661	1 skein
Bright Peacock Blue	835	660	1 skein
Sea Green	403	611	2 skeins
Sea Green	401	613	2 skeins
Sea Green	407	660	3 skeins
Cornflower	462	544	6 skeins

THE EHRMAN NEEDLEPOINT BOOK

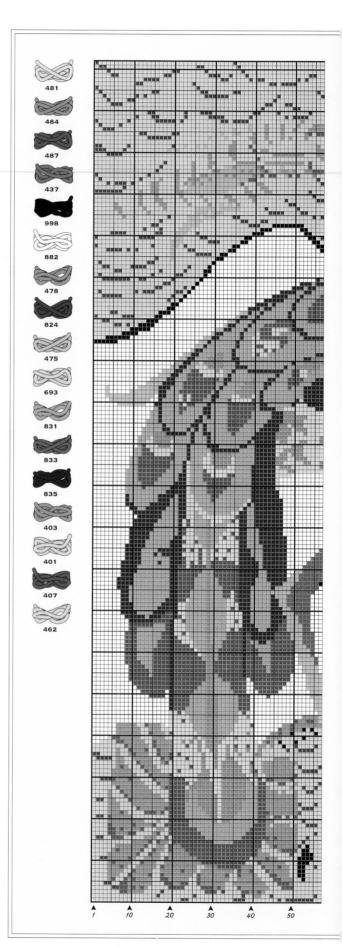

60 70 80 90 100 110 120 130 140 150 160 170 180 190 200 206

LINER

It is refreshing to be ending this chapter with Mike Wade's 'Liner'. It is a completely different subject and is Mike's first design for us. Mike is a graphic designer by trade and this comes across in the poster-like quality of his colour block composition. I always associate cruises with the P&O or Cunard liners of the interwar years, and the image is the image of the poster. Mike captures this with those limpid reflections and smoke trailing from the funnels; full moons, blue lagoons, white tuxedos, martinis – a Hollywood world of escape. We have photographed it as a picture as it seemed the most obvious format, but it could make a rather stylish long cushion for a high-backed chair.

As a company we have always encouraged designers unfamiliar with needlework to give it a go. I learnt last year that the architect Vanbrugh's first building was Castle Howard. Until then his design experience was limited to stage sets. An extreme example perhaps of the inspired amateurism of that age but something of this spirit needs to be recaptured. We live in an age which lays too great a store by qualifications. We are intimidated by this reverential respect for titles from wandering into fields which may interest us but of which we have little practical experience. At the end of the day you can't teach style and flair. Technical skills need to be thoroughly mastered, that goes without saying, but technical skill alone has never made great art. Our best designers like to work in a variety of materials. This is because they have a lot to say and different jobs require different tools. Look at Kaffe Fassett for example – a knitter, stitcher and painter who makes rag rugs and designs complex repeat fabric and wallpaper patterns for mechanical production. He has a sound technical understanding of how to work in all these disciplines and will suggest modifications to machinery or production processes to achieve the

result he is looking for. I am delighted that Peter Blake, the artist, should be designing for us and that we have a cushion in this book by Caroline Charles the fashion designer. The more involvement from outside, the more experimentation and the more cross-fertilisation of ideas that we can bring to the world of needlework the better. Let serendipity thrive.

Many of these new ideas prove to be uncommercial but you can never tell which ones will catch on till you have tried them. Kaffe Fassett's 'Cabbage' and 'Cauliflower' were wonderful designs but we thought they would probably be of limited appeal. They were our best-selling designs for over two years. That sort of unexpected success gives everyone a boost and encourages us to believe that the scope of needlework design can be widened.

As needlework in general declined after the war the commercial end narrowed its design focus on to what seemed safe. That is the familiar path of a declining trade starved of cash and sympathy. Fear and disillusion then feed on themselves. There was less to stitch so there were fewer stitchers. With fewer stitchers there was even greater caution when producing new design as the leeway for error kept diminishing. It takes a brand new approach to break out of this sort of cycle of decline. The needlework trade got it in the late 1970s with the arrival of Kaffe Fassett. His input has led to the total transformation we see today. He made it an interesting subject to work in again and as more stitchers were attracted so were more designers. When we started our business in 1978 the only other 'design-based' company was Glorafilia. At that time there were probably under a hundred needlepoint kits to stitch in this country. On my last visit to Liberty's needlework department I stopped counting after eight hundred. Times have certainly changed and a large measure of credit for this should go to Kaffe.

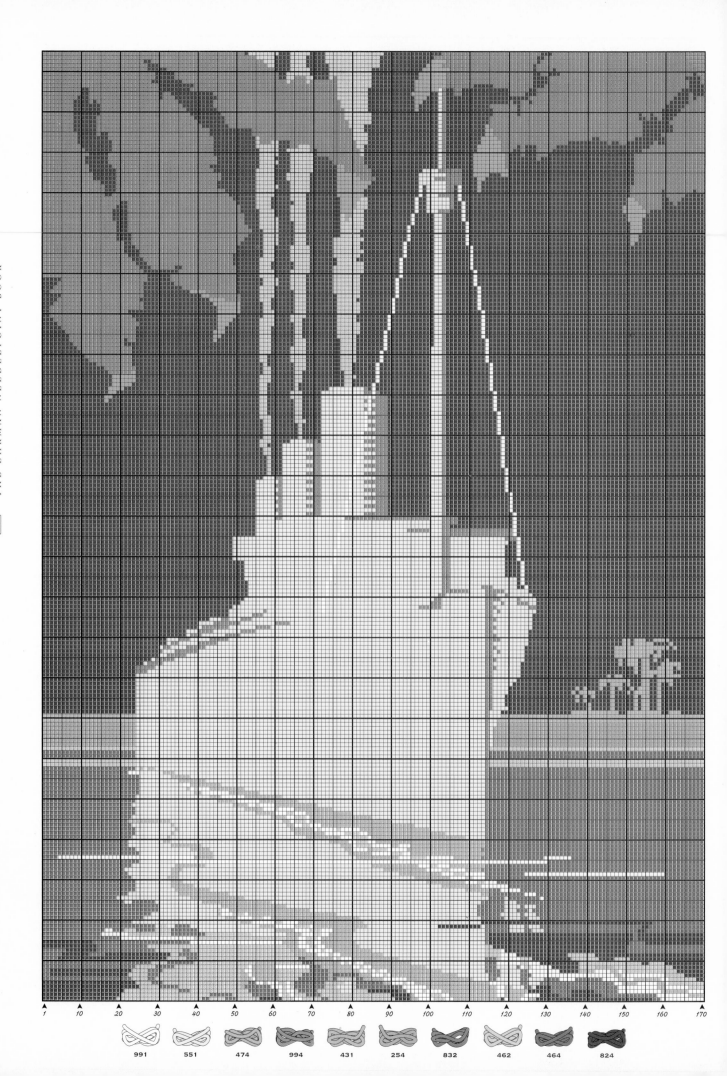

1   10   20   30   40   50   60   70   80   90   100   110   120   130   140   150   160   170

991   551   474   994   431   254   832   462   464   824

When we started our business the majority of the other kits around were for pictures. On the whole they were pretty awful: horses on the village green, Pierrots with tears running down their cheeks and a host of last suppers. I'm delighted to say that there are fewer of them around today. Needlepoint kits have gradually shifted in emphasis from stitched pictures to cushion covers, rugs and chairseats. Rex the friendly alsatian and semi-clad flamenco dancers may be in retreat but a gap has been left for more 'tasteful' pictures. There was never anything wrong with the idea of needlepoint pictures per se, it was just the subjects that were chosen and their crude colouring. Mike's 'Liner' is certainly something new. A number of Jill Gordon's recent cushion designs would work equally well as pictures, her landscapes in particular, and I suspect we may see a revival of stitched pictures. They are, after all, only smaller-scale hangings.

CANVAS: 12 holes to the inch

STITCH: Half-cross or tent

DESIGN AREA: 20in × 14½in (51cm × 37cm)

YARN: Appleton Tapestry wool or Paternayan

Shade	Appleton	Paternayan	
Royal Blue	824	540	17 skeins
Cornflower	464	542	5 skeins
Cornflower	462	544	3 skeins
Bright Peacock Blue	832	662	5 skeins
Grass Green	254	692	1 skein
Autumn Yellow	474	725	1 skein
Rust	994	852	3 skeins
Signal Green	431	687	2 skeins
Bright Yellow	551	773	9 skeins
White	991	261	2 skeins

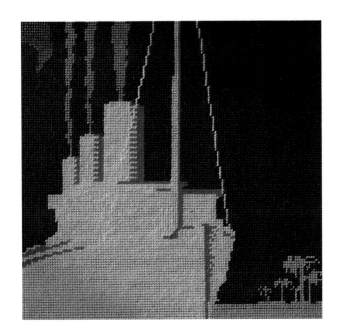

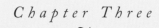

Chapter Three

~

NEW FLORALS

"There is no climate, no place, and scarcely an hour, in which nature does not exhibit colour which no mortal effort can imitate or approach. For all our artificial pigments are, even when seen under the same circumstances, dead and lightless beside her living colour; nature exhibits her hues under an intensity of sunlight which trebles their brilliancy."

JOHN RUSKIN, *MODERN PAINTERS*, 1843

POSY OF FLOWERS

Elian McCready's flowers glow with a burnished radiance that lifts the spirits. This chapter is largely devoted to them and it celebrates her joyous use of high colour. These flowers are usually on a large scale, leaping out of the picture at you, and they transmit Elian's sheer delight in her subject.

Colour is about stirring the emotions. When Chardin saw a fruit the visual experience filled him with such enjoyment that it invested eye and hand with the capacity to paint as he did. When Pieter de Hooch painted the roof of a house he conveyed to the spectator his own delight in the marvel of light, the wealth of colours and the tones that he saw.

The artist has to be moved for us to be, and Elian clearly is. Lecturing on colour in 1802, Henri Fuseli compared the eye's appreciation of colour to the ear's appreciation of music. 'Stern and deep-toned tints rouse, determine, invigorate the eye, as warlike sound or a deep bass the ear; and

bland, rosy, gray or vernal tints, smooth, calm or melt like a sweet melody.' A little contrived perhaps, but the analogy with music is often made by painters. David Hockney talks of tone being like pitch in music; and the combinations of tones to create a general colour effect could be compared to the combination of notes to create a single chord. After so much talk of painting with wool it is rather nice to think of composing with wool for a change.

Elian, like Kaffe Fassett and Jill Gordon, builds her compositions gradually, stitching her way forward. Colours are blended to build shaded pattern, and pyramids of colour gradually emerge by a progressive heightening of colour intensity. It is a process which requires constant refinements, changes of direction and experiments along the way.

Elian's method of stitching is tactile and immediate and this requires a knowledge of and feel for her ingredients – coloured wools. It is the way she blends and mixes them at each stage that determines the eventual outcome. That is why she can produce such highly-coloured designs which are, at the same time, so subtle. The colours build gradually. However bright her work it is never garish because colour is not thrown down in primary blocks. By constantly mixing her shades Elian 'paints' or 'composes' her creations! Strictly speaking what she does not do is 'design' them. Design implies a preconceived blueprint which is then executed. One thinks of designing a car or an alarm clock. Designers will often talk of 'resolving a problem' or of 'design solutions'. Elian's method is far more artistic in the sense that an artist lets the work, to a certain extent, evolve. She starts with a general idea of what she wants to achieve and draws a rough outline on to the canvas. The colour, with all that implies – shadow, perspective, depth – follows, and that determines the true character of her work.

CANVAS: 10 holes to the inch

STITCH: Half-cross or tent

DESIGN AREA: 16in × 16in (41cm × 41cm)

YARN: Appleton Tapestry wool or Paternayan

Shade	Appleton	Paternayan	
White	991	261	3 skeins
Off White	992	263	4 skeins
Mid Blue	156	532	2 skeins
Peacock Blue	643	602	2 skeins
Peacock Blue	642	D546	2 skeins
Grey Green	352	605	2 skeins
Dull Mauve	935	D115	2 skeins
Bright Rose Pink	941	934	3 skeins
Bright Rose Pink	943	932	2 skeins
Bright Rose Pink	944	904	3 skeins
Bright Rose Pink	946	903	2 skeins
Coral	862	854	2 skeins
Coral	864	832	2 skeins
Bright Mauve	451	323	2 skeins
Bright Mauve	453	302	2 skeins
Fuchsia	801	353	2 skeins
Fuchsia	805	350	2 skeins
Wine Red	716	910	3 skeins
Bright Rose Pink	948	901	3 skeins
Hyacinth	895	310	1 skein
Bright Yellow	551	773	2 skeins
Bright Yellow	554	771	2 skeins
Bright China Blue	741	564	1 skein

For many years Elian worked with Kaffe Fassett and for those of you who remember his 'Flower Trellis' rug the bold composition of these flowers will have a familiar look. Her flowers are always powerful. The scale of them in this design would, I think, allow for a border if you wanted to create a larger cushion. Maybe a geometric pattern using the same colours she has or perhaps a more fluid repeat pattern.

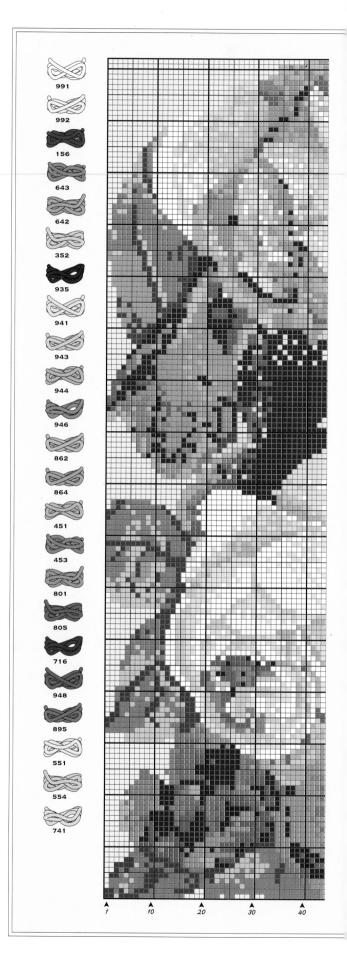

LILIES

A s you can see from Zöe and Tim Hill's luxuriant-ly rich photograph on the following page, the 'Lilies' and 'Nasturtiums' work as a colour group. They were designed by Elian McCready in the same year. The oranges and burnt sienna smoulder against her azure blue skies. The blue backing of 'Nasturtiums', in particular, is the blue of intense cobalt – a saturated French blue we rarely see in this country. These designs are shafts of sun-light that would cheer up any room.

'Lilies' is a standard-size cushion cover while 'Nasturtiums', stitched on the same ten mesh canvas, is larger, measuring 20in × 20in (51cm × 51cm). The panel looks far larger still but is actually 30in × 30in (76cm × 76cm). It is the way it is stitched which adds to the impression of size. It is worked in random long-stitch which gives the surface its silky tex-ture and a feeling of depth. Unfortunately this type of long-stitch is only suitable for canvases that are destined for the wall. Cushions or chairseats worked in this way would quickly fray and pull out of shape. Elian worked for many years with Kaffe Fassett and it was a method of stitching he adapted and developed for his large, commissioned hang-ings. It is quicker to work and gives a more fluid, 'painterly' feel to the design. The kit comes with a pre-printed colour canvas so you don't have to work from a chart. Elian has now completed a series of four floral hangings, this being the last. The first, 'Pansies', has proved to be the most pop-ular so far but I would not be surprised if 'Nasturtiums' ran it a close second. It is certainly one of her best.

NASTURTIUMS

Elian was originally a painter and it shows. She has a painter's eye for colour shading, like Jill Gordon and Kaffe Fassett, and any similarities that are still visible in their approach to needlework design are not coincidental. They have all worked together at one time or another. In the mid-1970s Kaffe set up a co-operative workshop in Gloucestershire with Lillian Delevoryas (Lillian now lives in America but examples of her work can be found in our earlier catalogues). It was called the Weatherall workshops and among those resident were Jill Gordon and Sarah Windrum, both of whom are designers we work with regularly. When the workshop closed and Kaffe moved back to London something of this spirit returned with him and throughout the 1980s a fluctuating

group of stitchers and designers gathered around him to help on his many projects. The most regular of these were Jill Gordon and Elian McCready and a whole school of design, based around Kaffe, emerged. They have now both gone their separate ways producing their own designs. Sadly we have only one of Jill's, 'Savonnèrie', in this book on page 123. She publishes her own book this year and quite correctly has reserved all her new work for it. It is a magnificent collection and many of these new designs will be in our 1996 catalogue. Elian also concentrates entirely on her own work these days which gets better and better. Luckily she did not have a book coming out this year! This trio of designs from her are among the best in the book and I am delighted that we have the space to do them justice.

This is primarily an exercise in shading but it was also the first design to use sky, and a descending depth of colour, for the background. All of Elian's previous designs had simple coloured backgrounds (where there was a background at all). The sky adds perspective and with it a new dimension to the whole design. Jill Gordon used descending tones of blue as a background for a firescreen of butterflies she stitched recently. It is most effective, drawing you into the picture. Here is a useful design tip, particularly for designs with a limited area of background. It immediately alters the character of the composition and gives it a lift.

CANVAS: 10 holes to the inch

STITCH: Half-cross or tent

DESIGN AREA: 16in × 16in (41cm × 41cm)

YARN: Appleton Tapestry wool or Paternayan

Shade	Appleton	Paternayan	
Dull Rose Pink	148	900	1 skein
Brown Olive	312	D531	2 skeins
Dull Marine Blue	327	510	2 skeins
Grey Green	353	604	2 skeins
Cornflower	461	564	4 skeins
Autumn Yellow	474	725	2 skeins
Scarlet	504	950	3 skeins
Turquoise	527	D502	2 skeins
Bright Yellow	553	772	2 skeins
Bright Yellow	557	812	2 skeins
Sky Blue	564	584	2 skeins
Mauve	606	310	1 skein
Royal Blue	822	542	3 skeins
Bright Peacock Blue	832	662	2 skeins
Coral	864	832	6 skeins
Pastel Lilac	885	313	1 skein
White	991	261	2 skeins
Rust	994	852	6 skeins
Lemon	996	673	2 skeins
Lime	997	672	1 skein
Charcoal	998	221	1 skein

PREVIOUS PAGES: THE FORCE OF ELIAN MCCREADY'S FLOWERS IS PARTLY A MATTER OF SCALE. THEY BURST FROM THE CANVAS. IT IS ALSO A MATTER OF COLOUR – A MARVELLOUS EVOCATION OF TROPICAL SUN AND DEEP SUMMER SKIES. THE 'NASTURTIUMS' CUSHION WAS STITCHED LATER TO ACCOMPANY THE LONG-STITCH PANEL

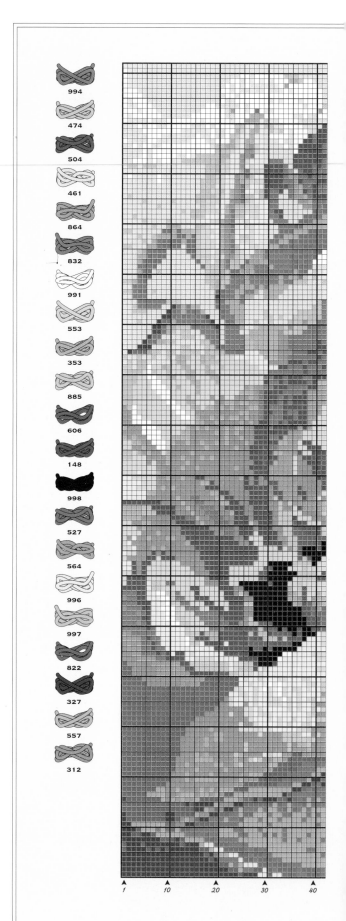

994
474
504
461
864
832
991
553
353
885
606
148
998
527
564
996
997
822
327
557
312

1 10 20 30 40

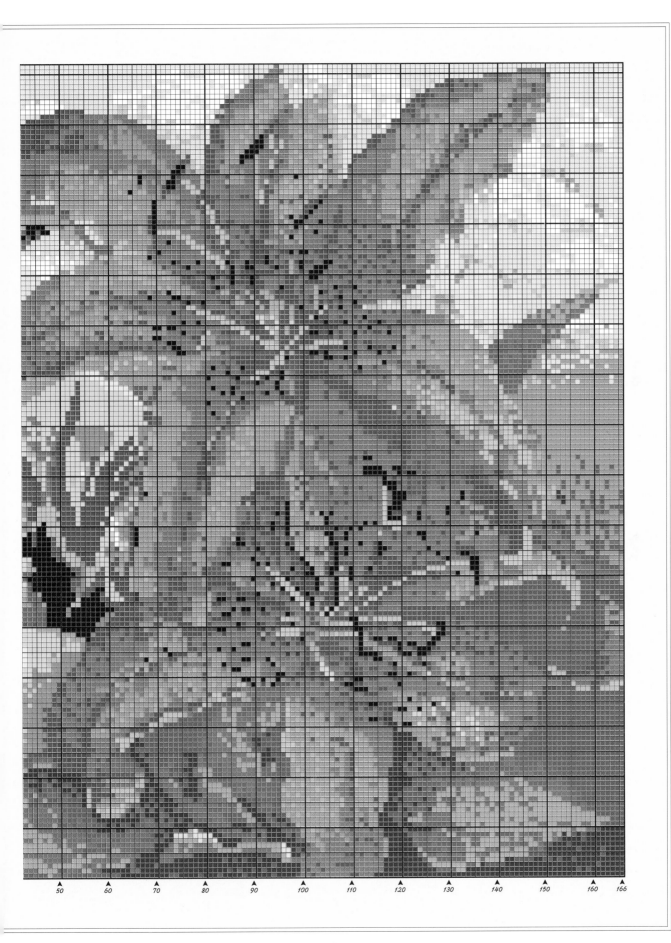

50 60 70 80 90 100 110 120 130 140 150 160 166

Elian combines really strong colours to glorious effect. Her innate sense of colour balance never lets her down even when she is testing the upper limits of the chromatic Richter scale.

CANVAS: 10 holes to the inch

STITCH: Half-cross or tent

DESIGN AREA: 20in × 20in (51cm × 51cm)

YARN: Paternayan

Shade	Paternayan	
Plum	320	2 skeins
Damson	900	3 skeins
Plum	321	2 skeins
Cherry Red	840	4 skeins
Burnt Sienna	852	5 skeins
Cherry Red	842	4 skeins
Orange	832	3 skeins
Yellow	812	4 skeins
Yellow	815	3 skeins
Butterscotch	702	2 skeins
Bright Yellow	712	2 skeins
Pale Yellow	727	2 skeins
Plum	322	1 skein
Plum	324	1 skein
Cobalt Blue	541	4 skeins
Bright Lime	671	2 skeins
Pine Green	531	1 skein
Peacock Green	520	2 skeins
Pine Green	532	2 skeins
Peacock Green	521	4 skeins
Peacock Green	522	5 skeins

60 70 80 90 100 110 120 130 140 150 160 170 180 190 200 210

GREEN NOSEGAY

Kaffe Fassett's voyages to the outer limits of neon colour were greeted by many with horror. It seemed a betrayal of all those years spent educating popular taste in an appreciation of soft, pastel shades. It was like Bob Dylan going electric! But others loved it; and for the past three or four years Kaffe has been experimenting, intermittently, with luminous, shock contrasts. As usual he was simply moving ahead of the times. You only have to look at modern furnishing fabrics or a copy of *Elle Decoration* to see how others have caught up. As we have become more used to seeing these dramatic hues around us the level of complaint that we receive about Kaffe's 'unnatural use of colour' has diminished correspondingly.

Natural colour is something of a myth, at least in painting. What any artist does with colour is personal and is to some extent unnatural. A natural use of colour is extremely rare in the history of art, and as the experiments of Turner and the Impressionists showed, extremely difficult to determine. When we see the real colours in nature we are apt to complain about their unreality. Kaffe is always keen to point out that colours in nature are often far stronger than we imagine. Look at some flowers close-up and you will find them astonishingly bright. In nature, however, they are toned down by the far larger areas of duller colours that surround them.

The overall design of Kaffe's 'Green Nosegay' is so electric because of the decorative framework Kaffe chooses for the pattern. Kaffe has taken strong, natural colours for the flowers and surrounded them with an unnatural continuation of the same, and that is why it looks so unusual. His confidence with really bright colour is unique and I wanted to feature this design for that reason. The original 'Ribbon Nosegay' was worked on a plum-coloured background which somehow flattened the design. Kaffe was unhappy with it and decided on a new approach. By placing it on this day-glo, grass green the whole thing comes to life and suddenly all these bright colours look good together. This is one of the rare Kaffe Fassett designs that is stitched on twelve holes to the inch canvas to capture the detail. The inspiration for this cushion was one of Kaffe's own waistcoats, stitched in petit-point, with a luscious combination of fruits and flowers. After the large dimensions of Elian McCready's 'Lilies' and 'Nasturtiums' it is nice to have some stitched on a smaller scale.

DIZZY COLOURS FROM THE WORLD'S MOST
ADVENTUROUS STITCHER. KAFFE FASSETT IS ALWAYS MOVING ON.
BY THE TIME PEOPLE HAVE GOT USED TO ONE STYLE
HE IS ALREADY WORKING ON THE NEXT

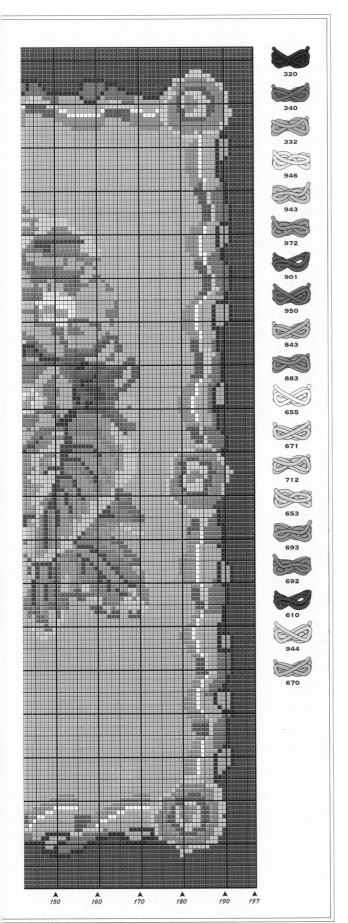

If the border or green background were not to your taste the central group of flowers could be used in a number of ways. I think the combination of the bright green with the high colours of the flowers is the essence of this design but I can see that the end product may be too strong for some people's furnishings. If that is so don't just pass this design by. The flowers could be set against a black or French blue background (like Elian McCready's 'Nasturtiums' background) for a totally different effect. Stitched in this way it could make a lively, smaller cushion with the outer leaves and petals stretching to the edge of the canvas. Bordered with braiding or cord it would measure roughly twelve or thirteen inches square; or it could then be set in a wider fabric border.

CANVAS: 12 holes to the inch

STITCH: Half-cross or tent

DESIGN AREA: 16in × 16in (41cm × 41cm)

YARN: Paternayan

Shade	Paternayan	
Bright Lime	670	8 skeins
Plum	320	1 skein
Pale Violet	340	1 skein
Bright Lavender	332	2 skeins
Pink	946	1 skein
Pink	943	1 skein
Scarlet	972	2 skeins
Damson	901	2 skeins
Strawberry	950	1 skein
Cherry Red	843	1 skein
Ginger Brown	883	1 skein
Jade Green	655	1 skein
Bright Lime	671	1 skein
Bright Yellow	712	1 skein
Jade Green	653	2 skeins
Leaf Green	693	1 skein
Leaf Green	692	2 skeins
Hunter Green	610	5 skeins
Pink	944	1 skein

FOXGLOVES AND
DELPHINIUMS

After the wild and colourful intoxication of the past sixteen pages we are given a breather with Ann Blockley's pair of hangings.

Ingres's advice to Degas to 'Draw lines, many lines, from memory or nature; it is by this that you will become a good artist' applies particularly to botanical drawing. It is endless observation, not an adherence to mathematical principles, that lies at the heart of successful flower painting. Ann Blockley is a watercolourist and her two panels capture the washed feel of watercolour. This is especially true of the abstract backgrounds. The foxgloves and delphiniums are drawn with a practised eye and although she presented the artwork on graph paper, with each stitched square marked out, she has managed to retain the dynamic of her original watercolour paintings. In some ways they remind me of Japanese screen panels or Chinese scroll paintings with their long, thin dimensions and focus on individual flowers.

In the East the tradition of painting flowers from natural observation had religious origins. In China, Buddhist art was a powerful stimulus to flower painting. The demand for flower-filled skies in paradise scenes and for flower borders on religious banners and wallpaintings prompted painters to study floral form in detail. In the case of Japan we think of the traditional folding screens decorated with plants, bamboo or flowers. Flower studies in the West had medicinal rather than religious origins. Italian and German herbal books of the fourteenth century used material rediscovered in the first century volumes of the Greek medical expert Dioscorides. They are remarkably similar to studies of fruits and flowers found in the pattern books of the early fifteenth-century tapestry weavers. This western tradition of natural study reached its apotheosis in the late fifteenth century with Albrecht Dürer's hyper-realistic depictions of animals, flowers and plant life.

The study of individual flowers is common to all parts of the world. People have always had an irrepressible imperative to record the world they find around, but the study of individual flowers has something else: a delight in form and colour for its own sake. Flowers are surely one of the wonders of the world and we are driven to paint, stitch and photograph them. We simply can't help it, they are irresistible, and every generation of artist at some stage has a go.

I first saw Ann's work in *Country Living* magazine. They had a pair of her paintings, watercolours of geese and pheasants, which I thought could make good needlepoint designs. She was interested in the idea and over the next two or three years went on to produce a series of five kits all based on farmyard animals, or animals native to Gloucestershire where she lives. Her 'Geese' were particularly popular. But five was enough and she wanted a change! The idea of these two panels was entirely her own and she regards them as more truly her own work. I think they have worked-up very successfully and add something fresh and different to our collection. Her choice of foxgloves and delphiniums and their unembellished presentation (no stylised borders or motifs) gives these designs a natural, 'cottagey' feel.

The background drifts of colour involve numerous colour changes. However, the odd misplaced stitch will make no difference to the finished piece. Shading of this subtlety is only achieved by blending tones, almost stitch by stitch, and when working the printed canvas from one of our kits it is inevitable that one or two stitches will be unclear. It doesn't matter. The nature of these designs implies a certain irregularity and it is the irregularity of needlework which is part of its charm. You are not stitching straight lines here and the message from all our designers is to relax and enjoy it.

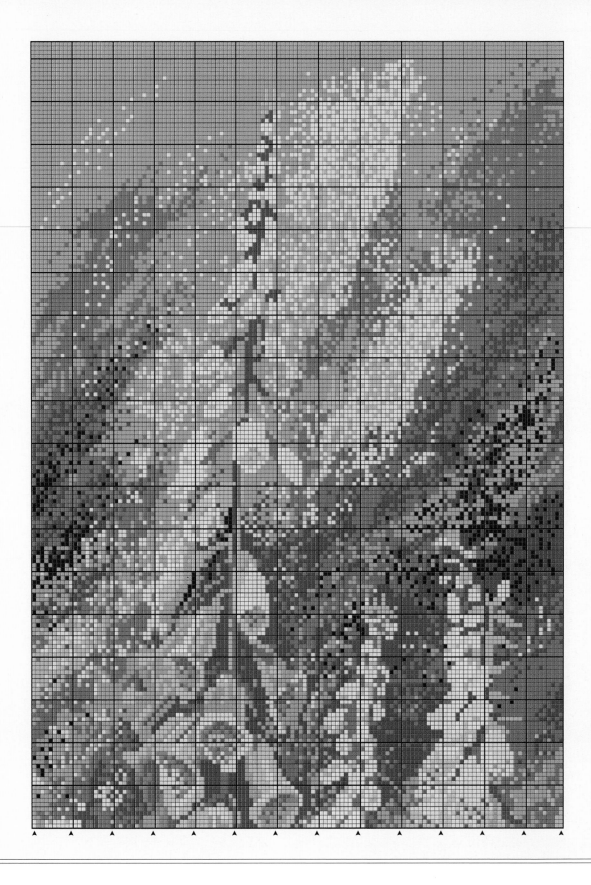

CANVAS: 10 holes to the inch

STITCH: Half-cross or tent

DESIGN AREA: 37in × 13in (93cm × 33cm)

YARN: Anchor Tapisserie or Paternayan

Shade	Anchor	Paternayan	
Autumn Gold	8054	754	3 skeins
Laurel	9002	663	6 skeins
Forest Green	9020	602	11 skeins
Forest Green	9022	600	8 skeins
Sea Green	8904	510	2 skeins

8054
9002
9020
9022
8904
8924
8894
8898
8542
8412
8414
8418
8508

Shade	Anchor	Paternayan		Shade	Anchor	Paternayan	
Peacock Green	8924	521	3 skeins	Raspberry	8412	901	5 skeins
Sea Green	8894	203	5 skeins	Raspberry	8414	901	4 skeins
Sea Green	8898	514	9 skeins	Raspberry	8418	912	2 skeins
Lavender	8542	323	4 skeins	Damson	8508	922	3 skeins

CANVAS: 10 holes to the inch			
STITCH: Half-cross or tent			
DESIGN AREA: 37in × 13in (93cm × 33cm)			
YARN: Anchor Tapisserie or Paternayan			

Shade	*Anchor*	*Paternayan*	
Spruce Green	9080	600	5 skeins
Spruce Green	9078	601	5 skeins
Spruce Green	9076	602	8 skeins
Sea Green	8896	514	10 skeins
Periwinkle	8610	341	2 skeins

Shade	Anchor	Paternayan		Shade	Anchor	Paternayan	
Periwinkle	8608	342	3 skeins	Moss Green	9214	694	3 skeins
Periwinkle	8604	343	2 skeins	Sage Green	9256	644	4 skeins
Steel Grey	8714	213	3 skeins	Cream	8006	263	3 skeins
Cinnamon	9388	442	5 skeins	Sea Green	8898	533	2 skeins

FRUIT DROPS

We end the chapter as we started it with a fiery blaze of Elian McCready colour. This is not a floral design but it seemed the only appropriate chapter for it. Fruits and flowers go well together. We have only two designs based on fruit in the whole book, this one and Neil McCallum's 'Chalice of Fruit' in the last chapter. This is surprising really as for two or three years our catalogue was like a greengrocer's stall. Elian was very much part of that process. She was working with Kaffe Fassett at the time and he was primarily responsible for the fructification of our range. There is no doubt that she learnt a lot from his fruit stitching technique. Her 'Fruit Drops' have the same lustrous quality that Kaffe gets into his pears, apples, plums and lemons. In his memorable 'Apple and Cabbage' carpet Kaffe groups fruits and vegetables with a generous profusion but his cushion-cover kits tended to be single studies: cherries, melons, plums. Their bold scale was part of their success. Here Elian stitches her fruits in a similar way, mixing wools to paint highlights, but uses them as elements grouped within an overall composition. On this smaller scale she still manages to evoke a skilful impression of their surface texture.

The colour balance is similar to her earlier group. An effulgent cocktail of glimmering embers, with brighter sparks of pink, yellow and crimson, shines from a blue backdrop. In this case a darker blue. The speckled background adds a new element – a touch of jollity – while balancing the design. Here is another familiar Kaffe Fassett/Elian McCready touch. I remember a spectacular chair Kaffe stitched for Sonia Rykiel with fruits and flowers on a black background sprayed with white dots. It lifts the design and can generally be a useful device for backgrounds which need a bit of spicing up.

The art historian and poet Herbert Read divided the use of colour in painting into three general categories: the 'heraldic', the 'harmonic' and the 'pure.' The heraldic was the most primitive and died out in the Middle Ages. Colour was used for symbolic significance and was static, so the robe of the Virgin must always be blue, her cloak red

and so on. The harmonic was the next stage where tonal values and relative intensity involved regulating the colours to conform to a restricted scale. A dominant tone was selected and all other colours were scaled up or down to a restricted distance from this scale. The general practice from the sixteenth to the eighteenth century was to work from a scaled palette, your colours neatly laid out within a narrow range. A perfect example of the harmonic use of colour would be the Dutch painter Van Goyen. In quite separate ways both Turner and Constable rebelled against this tradition and formed a bridge to the later world of pure colour. Here colour was used for its own sake – Matisse being the most obvious example this century. Colours are taken in their purest intensity and pattern is built up in contrasts of relative intensity. As the main purpose is decorative, questions of verisimilitude are secondary. Colour is reduced to its most direct, sensuous appeal. Looked at in this way colour has always been in the eye of the beholder or more exactly in the imagination of the beholder, and the brighter colours we see in this chapter justify the title 'New Florals.' They are clearly coloured in what Herbert Read would term the 'pure' manner and appeal, unashamedly, on a sensuous and decorative level.

This chapter has been about shading, stitching graded dots of colour to build an image. There are many other needlework techniques for designing flowers. In the first chapter we saw the 'Berlin Roses'. These were adapted from Berlin Woolwork charts which built up petals and leaves with an almost photographic precision. They used a lot of colours and a fine gauge of canvas to achieve an equally subtle result. But the design technique was quite different. It depended on contrasting shades of light with shadow to define colour blocks. It was a more graphic approach to

FRUITS AND LEAVES FROM ELIAN ON A SMALLER SCALE THAN
USUAL BUT WITH A FAMILIAR INTENSITY OF HIGH COLOURS
SET THIS TIME ON A SPOTTED BACKGROUND

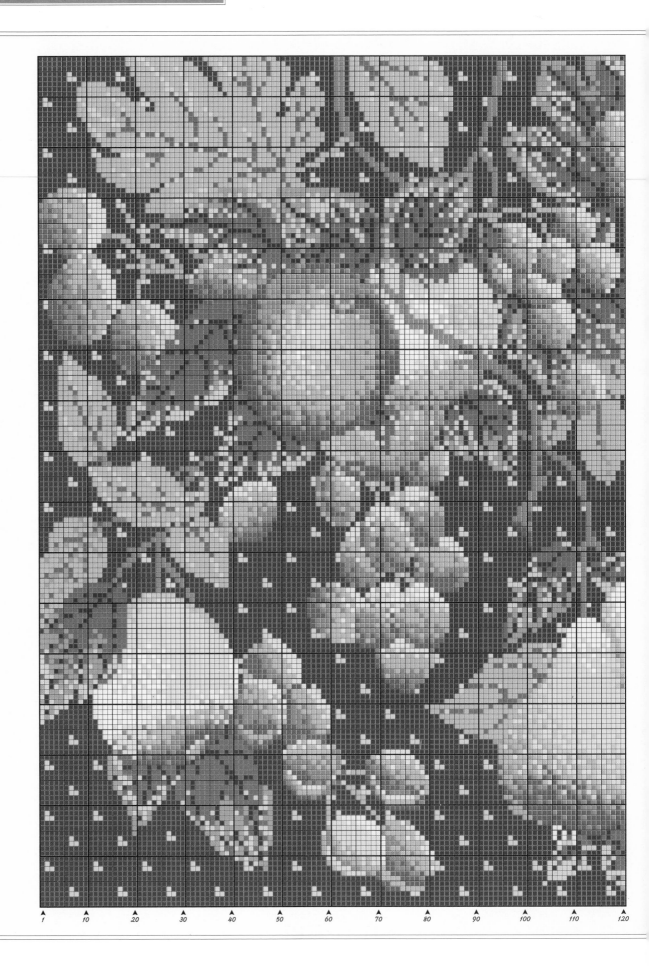

1 10 20 30 40 50 60 70 80 90 100 110 120

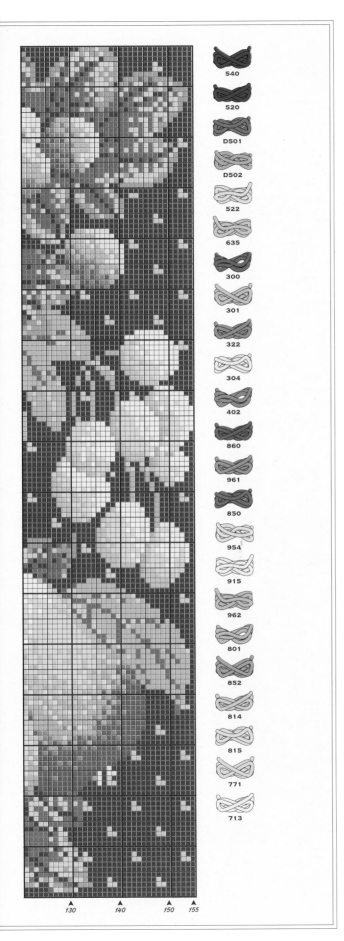

| 540 |
| 520 |
| D501 |
| D502 |
| 522 |
| 635 |
| 300 |
| 301 |
| 322 |
| 304 |
| 402 |
| 860 |
| 961 |
| 850 |
| 954 |
| 915 |
| 962 |
| 801 |
| 852 |
| 814 |
| 815 |
| 771 |
| 713 |

130   140   150 155

colour differentiation. The spring flowers in the 'Alphabet Cushion', at the start of Chapter 5, are simplified down to two or three colours for each flower. No technique is 'better' than any other, they can all be equally effective. What is true, however, is that the technique we have looked at in this chapter is unique. Kaffe Fassett, Elian McCready and Jill Gordon have developed a needlework technique of painting with wool which is entirely their own.

CANVAS: 10 holes to the inch

STITCH: Half-cross or tent

DESIGN AREA: $16\frac{1}{2}$in × $15\frac{1}{2}$in (42cm × 39cm)

YARN: Paternayan

Shade	Paternayan	
Cobalt Blue	540	8 skeins
Peacock Green	520	2 skeins
Turquoise	D501	3 skeins
Turquoise	D502	2 skeins
Peacock Green	522	2 skeins
Pale Spring Green	635	3 skeins
Purple	300	1 skein
Purple	301	2 skeins
Plum	322	2 skeins
Purple	304	1 skein
Brown	402	1 skein
Rust	860	1 skein
Bright Pink	961	1 skein
Burnt Sienna	850	1 skein
Strawberry	954	1 skein
Pale Pink	915	1 skein
Bright Pink	962	1 skein
Marigold	801	1 skein
Burnt Sienna	852	1 skein
Yellow	814	1 skein
Yellow	815	1 skein
Bright Yellow	771	2 skeins
Bright Yellow	713	1 skein

Drenched in the golden light of evening Elian's fruits are illuminated against the darkening sky. 'Blazing in Gold and quenching in Purple' is how the poet Emily Dickinson once described a sunset, and a similar drama is being enacted here on Elian's canvas.

Chapter Four

~

A LIGHTER TOUCH

"Humour is the great thing, the saving thing after all. The minute it crops up, all our hardnesses yield, all our irritations and resentments flit away, and a sunny spirit takes their place."

MARK TWAIN, FROM HIS ESSAY
WHAT PAUL BOURGET THINKS OF US, 1895

CROWN

The more demanding life becomes the more important it is to maintain a sense of proportion and a sense of humour. All of our designers have a good sense of humour, thank God, and none of them take themselves too seriously. A sense of the ridiculous often goes hand in hand with an enjoyment of the unexpected. In design terms this means a quick eye for a visual joke, a lively, enquiring mind and a healthy disdain for the obvious. This outlook is most commonly witnessed nowadays in advertising. Advertising often relies for its impact on taking a familiar situation and turning it on its head. It was difficult to think of a title for this chapter. All the designs have a touch of levity. The element of humour, for want of a better word, lies simply in the fact that they make you smile.

They are graphic and bold and focus on their subject matter. They have a lighter touch, a metaphorical spring in their step, and a sense of fun. Their common denominator is a *joie de vivre*, and what better design to kick off with than Caroline Charles's 'Crown'?

Contact was made with Caroline Charles via a mutual friend. I was a little surprised and quite delighted to hear that one of our top fashion designers was interested in designing a needlepoint kit with us. In fact she designed two, the 'Crown' and the 'Last Stitch', of which the 'Crown', I think, is the more successful. Her design department were very thorough, experimenting with a number of different combinations until they were satisfied. The design itself is punchy and stylish (as you would expect) but the

colours are beautifully judged with considerable thought going into their selection. The result is a cushion which is fun without being gimmicky and it will appeal to a whole new group of stitchers.

I am writing this on the day that Caroline is opening a new shop in Bond Street, London. What she describes as her fit, small business is going through a phase of fairly dramatic expansion. Along with her other shop in Beauchamp Place, London her burgeoning empire encompasses wholesaling and retailing with new ranges of bedlinen, shoes, sunglasses and bags as well as the clothes. Like Paul Smith (Britain's other most successful clothes designer) she is extending her lucrative Japanese licensing operation and is a consultant to Marks and Spencer. The secret of her success

CAROLINE CHARLES IS ONE OF BRITAIN'S LEADING FASHION DESIGNERS AND HERE SHE TURNS HER HAND TO NEEDLEPOINT FOR THE FIRST TIME. HUMOUR, VERVE AND PANACHE AS YOU WOULD EXPECT

is that she has a clear idea of where she is going and who her customers are. At a youthful-looking fifty she has a wealth of experience stretching back to the early sixties when she worked for Mary Quant. Her first collection was put together in London in 1963.

There has always been a connection with needlework. She started sewing at her convent school in Woldingham so that she could whip up a frock by speech day. Before Mary Quant she worked for Michael Sherrard in Curzon Street, London, where she learnt every sort of couture sewing technique. 'It was seventy per cent hand sewing; even the seams inside the linings were oversewn by hand.' Knowing this now I am far less surprised that she should have wanted to design a needlepoint kit. She loves the idea of anything new and has an infectious enthusiasm for whatever she is doing. We have tried working with fashion designers before but their designs did not succeed because they simply transferred fabric pattern onto canvas. Caroline designs a needlepoint as a needlepoint. She does not use needlework as a vehicle for extending a particular design style. Her work has a rigour and discipline which eschews such indulgence.

CANVAS: 12 holes to the inch

STITCH: Half-cross or tent

DESIGN AREA: 18in × 18in (46cm × 46cm)

YARN: Appleton Tapestry wool or Paternayan

Shade	Appleton	Paternayan	
Dark Damson Pink	948	901	2 skeins
Scarlet	501	951	3 skeins
Bright Rose Pink	946	903	1 skein
Charcoal	998	221	6 skeins
Putty Grounding	988	465	7 skeins
Sky Blue	568	500	4 skeins
Purple	106	312	1 skein
Early English Green	545	691	3 skeins
Grey Green	358	600	2 skeins
Autumn Yellow	474	725	5 skeins
Heraldic Gold	842	734	5 skeins
Off White	992	263	1 skein

This cushion is hard to classify. It is more masculine than most of our designs but with an element of camp; a bit of a joke but smart at the same time. Like so much that is stylish it is ambivalent and this gives it a wider potential audience. You could take the central section of the 'Crown', put it on a ten mesh canvas to make it a bit larger, and stitch it as a cut-out like Kaffe Fassett's 'Lily Pad Frog'. You could stitch a number of 'crowns' by themselves and experiment with different coloured backgrounds. I also think the tasselled border is rather good and could be used effectively on other designs. Being designed in clearly separated sections this is a good pattern for chopping, changing and having fun with: a designer's design to enjoy.

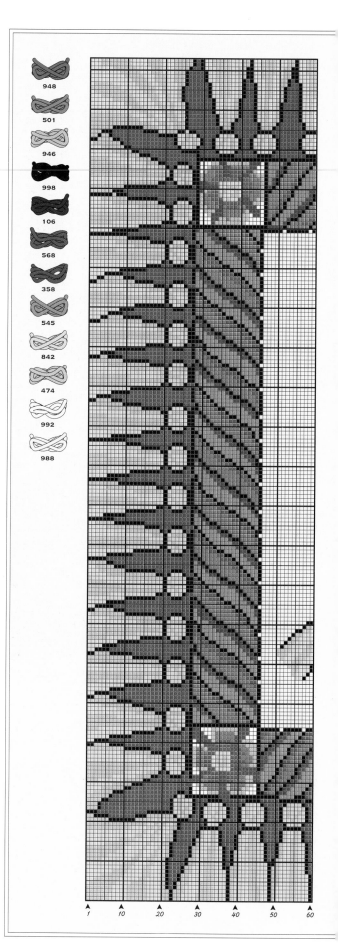

70 80 90 100 110 120 130 140 150 160 170 180 190 200 210 220

ALBION
AND
AMERICA

These two designs from Candace Bahouth are an interesting combination of the old and the new. There is the graphic, pop-art immediacy of the flag. But in both cases it is a flag of historical reference; a flag you would associate with the folk art of either country. It is most appropriate that they should have been designed by Candace – an American who has made her home in England – and they have all the style and charm that we have come to associate with her needlework.

Most countries in the world take a pride in their national flag, but in varying degrees. In Europe for example the French have a far stronger attachment to their Tricolour than the Germans have to theirs. The historical reasons are obvious and, in any case, the present German flag was only adopted in 1949. The British, like the French, have a deep rooted pride in their flag but, on the whole, it is an unobtrusive pride. These distinctions become marginal when compared with America. America is awash with Stars and Stripes from coast to coast. And the Americans' pride in their flag cuts across social, age and geographical division. When the anti-war protesters burnt their national flag in public in the 1960s it was a far more shocking act of defiance than it would have been in any European country. It would be almost impossible to spend a day anywhere in America without seeing at least one image of the Stars and Stripes. Flags don't just fly on public buildings. They fly in their hundreds of thousands (possibly millions) on flag poles erected in suburban gardens across the land. The

THE UNION JACK, BLOWING IN THE BREEZE, IS STITCHED BY CANDACE BAHOUTH, AN AMERICAN WHO HAS MADE HER HOME IN THE HEART OF THE ENGLISH COUNTRYSIDE NEAR GLASTONBURY IN SOMERSET

bicentennial celebrations brought home what a relatively new country America still is and the flag is a symbolic image of unity – the American way of life made flesh – for communities from all over the world making a new life together. As a British citizen owes allegiance to the throne, so an American owes allegiance to the flag. The flag binds. The 'Pledge to the Flag' is as follows: " I pledge allegiance to the flag of the United States of America, and to the Republic for which it stands, one nation under God, indivisible, with liberty and justice for all."

The British flag presented the greater problem. You have to be careful with the Union Jack these days. It is a sad fact that it has been partially hijacked by the extreme right and, used in the wrong way, can convey all the wrong sort of messages. A way around this was to return to a flag of historical reference, and if the cushions were to be designed as a pair it was the obvious thing to do anyway. Candace's British flag is based on one she found on a cigarette card and has the same fresh, breezy invigoration as its American counterpart.

The term 'Jack' was first used in the British Navy to describe the Union Flag that was, at that time, flown at the main masthead. It was an affectionate nickname meaning small, an ironic reference to the flag's large size. By the later seventeenth century the term had stuck and a vote in the Houses of Parliament in May 1660 refers to 'standards, fflags and Jacke colours of the ffleets'. In typically eccentric fashion the United Kingdom is one of the very few countries in the world which has no official national flag. The Union Flag officially remains the Sovereign's. It can, by common practice, be used by British subjects ashore but the Merchant Shipping Act of 1894 expressly forbids its use afloat. The flag itself is an amalgam of the national flags of England, Scotland and Ireland. St George became the patron saint of England in 1277 and his cross was first used as the emblem of England during the Welsh wars of Edward I. The origins of the Scottish flag go back further, as legend would have it, to AD736 when Angus, Son of Fergus, King of the Picts, adopted St Andrew as his patron saint. St Andrew had been crucified on a diagonal cross in AD 69. The cross of St George (red on a white ground) was joined by the white saltire (or diagonal) cross of St Andrew on its blue ground in 1603 when James I united the thrones of England and Scotland. The flag of St Patrick was added in 1801 with the incorporation of Ireland into the Union of Great Britain. The cross of St Patrick, like that of St George, is red on white but, like the cross of St Andrew, goes from corner to corner. The Union Jack, by sacrificing most of the white background, combines the distinctive features of all three.

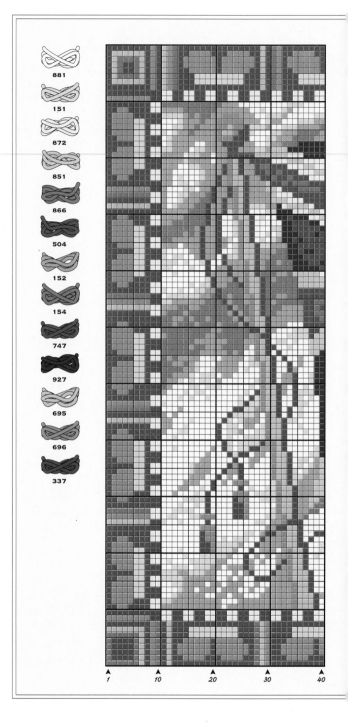

CANVAS: 10 holes to the inch

STITCH: Half-cross or tent

DESIGN area: 15½in × 11in (39cm × 28cm)

YARN: Appleton Tapestry wool or Paternayan

Shade	Appleton	Paternayan	
Pastel Cream	881	262	3 skeins
Mid Blue	151	203	2 skeins
Pastel Yellow	872	715	2 skeins
Custard Yellow	851	D541	2 skeins

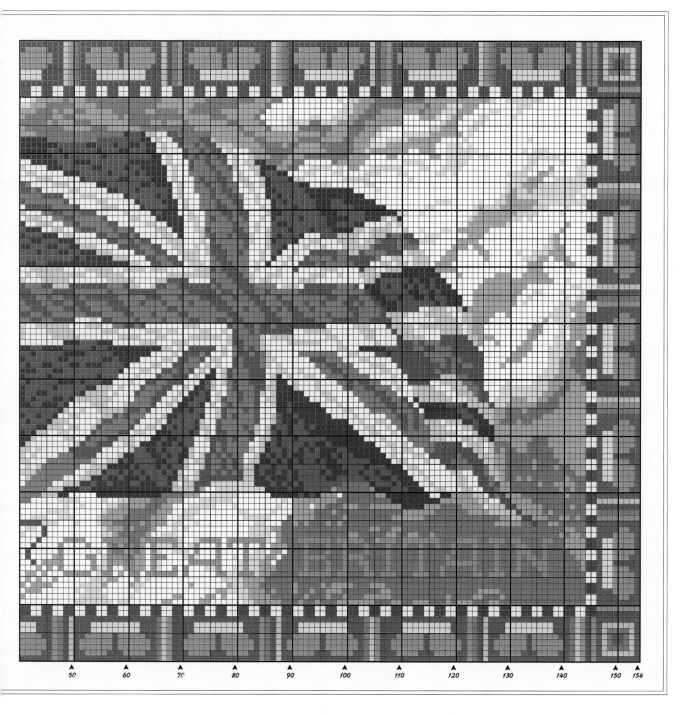

A LIGHTER TOUCH

Shade	Appleton	Paternayan	
Coral	866	850	2 skeins
Scarlet	504	950	2 skeins
Mid Blue	152	514	2 skeins
Mid Blue	154	534	2 skeins
Bright China Blue	747	500	2 skeins
Dull China Blue	927	510	2 skeins
Honeysuckle Yellow	695	732	1 skein
Honeysuckle Yellow	696	740	2 skeins
Drab Green	337	451	2 skeins

Flags are a splendid idea for needlepoint. We have started with the Union Jack and the Stars and Stripes as obvious choices but combinations of flags would look equally good. There are books of flags published where the flags are set out in series – naval, heraldic, regional. They would make excellent material for design. Most flags have fairly straight-forward blocks so would be simple to stitch. In groups they are both elegant and graphic. Albion's border gets lost here and it might be better to stitch out a little further so that it becomes more visible when the cushion is backed.

Both Candace and I had the idea for the American flag at about the same time. I had seen a wonderful nineteenth-century American fabric with the Stars and Stripes used as the main motif. Most versions of the American flag are flat: a two-dimensional graphic image. The flag on this nine-teenth-century fabric was fluttering in the wind. I started looking for pictures of old flags with a similar elegance and movement. At the same time Candace sent me a postcard from a museum in New England of an American flag, very much in the folk art tradition and suggested it as an idea for a needlepoint kit. We were clearly heading in the same direction and, working on a variety of source material, Candace soon produced this lovely version. It reminds me of the American flag you see in films as the US cavalry rides to the rescue.

The Stars and Stripes dates back to the Continental Congress of 14 June 1777 which "Resolved, that the Flag of the United States be thirteen stripes alternate red and white, that the Union be thirteen stars white on a blue field, representing a constellation". The colours, red, white and blue were adopted from the old colonial East India Company Ensign, which were themselves the same colours found in the British flag. The thirteen states of the original union stretched up the eastern seaboard from South Carolina to New Hampshire and as new states joined a new star would be added. They started by trying to increase the stripes as well but when the total reached eighteen it was clear that the flag would end up looking like a piece of shirting. So at the Congress of 4 April 1818 it was enacted that the stripes should be reduced permanently to the origi-nal thirteen with stars alone added as new states joined the union. The last star to be added was Hawaii's in July 1960.

O say can you see by the dawn's early light
What so proudly we hail'd at the twilight's last gleaming,
Whose broad stripes and bright stars through the perilous fight
O'er the ramparts we watch'd, were so gallantly streaming?
And the rocket's red glare, the bomb bursting in air,
Gave proof through the night that our flag was still there,
O say does that star-spangled banner yet wave
O'er the land of the free and the home of the brave?

The stirring first verse of 'The Star Spangled Banner' writ-ten by Francis Scott Key during the second American War of Independence in 1814. It marks the real beginning of national devotion to the flag and the patriotic song was officially adopted as the national anthem of the United States in March 1931.

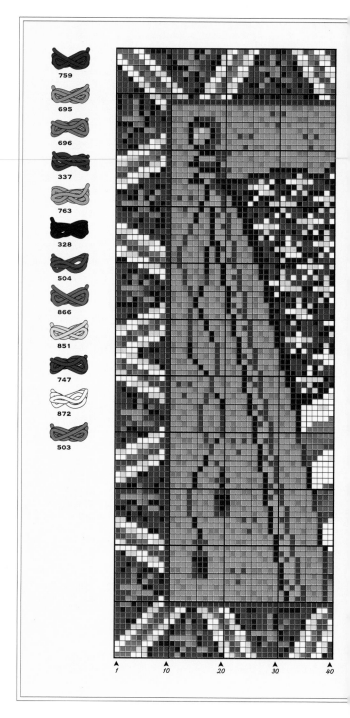

759
695
696
337
763
328
504
866
851
747
872
503

1   10   20   30   40

PREVIOUS PAGES: CANDACE STITCHES HER OWN NATION'S FLAG WITH LOVE, AFFECTION AND A PAINSTAKING ATTENTION TO DETAIL. SHE HAS COPED BRILLIANTLY WITH THE STARS, AND THE BACKGROUND COLOUR WAS WORKED AND REWORKED UNTIL SHE WAS HAPPY. THE ROPE AND TASSELS GIVE IT ITS PEDIGREE.

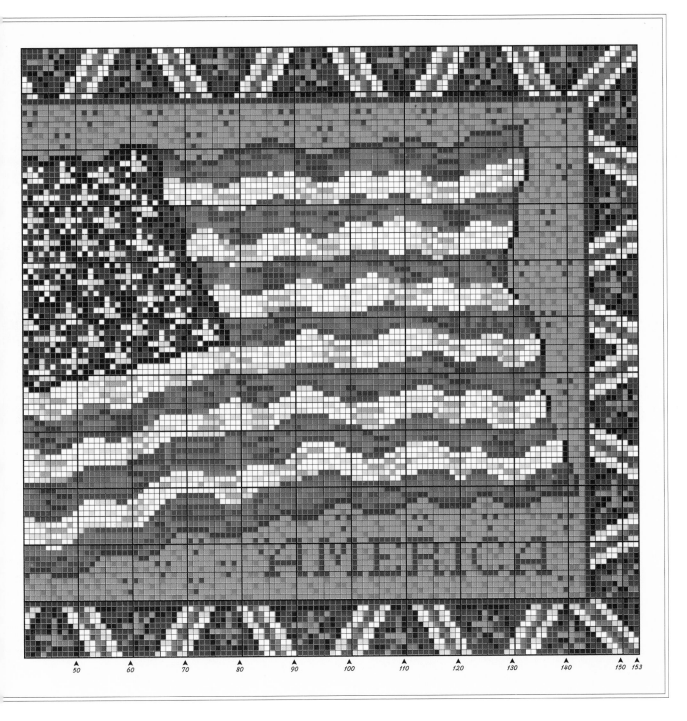

CANVAS: 10 holes to the inch

STITCH: Half-cross or tent

DESIGN AREA: 15½in × 11in (39cm × 28cm)

YARN: Appleton Tapestry wool or Paternayan

Shade	Appleton	Paternayan	
Rose Pink	759	900	2 skeins
Honeysuckle Yellow	695	732	5 skeins
Honeysuckle Yellow	696	740	2 skeins
Drab Green	337	451	2 skeins
Biscuit	763	434	1 skein
Bright China Blue	747	500	3 skeins
Scarlet	504	950	2 skeins
Coral	866	850	2 skeins
Custard Yellow	851	D541	2 skeins
Dull Marine Blue	328	510	3 skeins
Pastel Yellow	872	715	4 skeins
Scarlet	503	951	2 skeins

LILY PAD FROG

nbeknownst to themselves frogs and pigs are cult creatures. We have learnt this from experience. Requests for frogs and pigs to stitch top our list. They may not be overwhelming in numbers, these piggy and froggy folk, but they are passionate in pursuit of their subject. Frog freaks collect anything with a frog on it, and a similar ardour animates your swine-lover. So it was only a matter of time before Britain's leading animal stitcher should have a crack at one of them, and Kaffe Fassett went for the frog. What a dashing figure he cuts. Crouching in slippery splendour, poised to leap from his lily pad, he is a compressed coil of energy and must be one of Kaffe's most life-like creations. The shading and use of colour to evoke that lubricious sheen is a tour de force and the strong, bold outline could only be Kaffe's. He is stitched with an eloquent authority on eight holes to the inch canvas with only

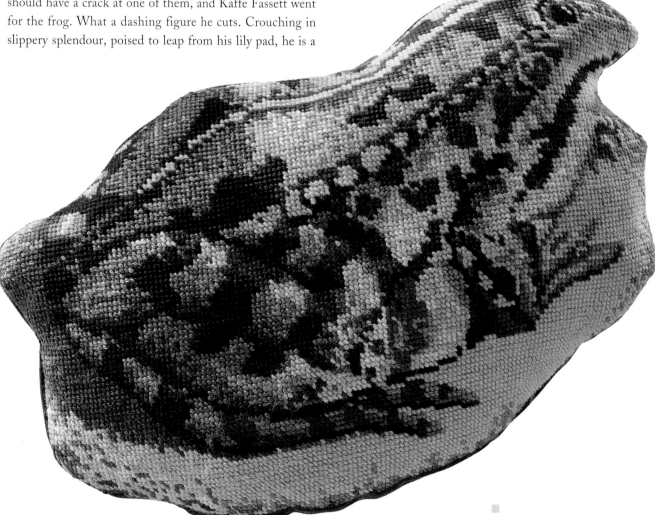

WITHOUT DOUBT A KAFFE FASSETT CLASSIC, A CONFIDENCE OF COLOUR AND SCALE WHICH SWEEPS ALL BEFORE IT. THIS FROG BREATHES ENERGY AND LIFE

eleven shades of wool. With so few colours on such a wide-gauged canvas this needlepoint shows, once again, that good design can be achieved with relative simplicity. It is the way you use your colours, not how many you have, that counts.

Why frogs and pigs? I don't really know. There is something appealing in their ugliness I suppose – like post-war French cars. It's the right sort of ugliness, an endearing ugliness, unlike bats or rats (although even they have their followings). Whatever it is frogs have risen a long way in public esteem. In religious paintings of the Middle Ages they symbolised sin. They were given a devilish significance and often likened to heretics. After all, one of the plagues of Egypt was a rain of frogs. But now we have Mr Jeremy Fisher, Kermit the Frog and the Frog Prince. The toad may have retained his malevolent reputation but the frog has become a perfectly respectable member of the animal kingdom. He certainly makes a fine subject for all sorts of artists and is particularly popular among jewellers and sculptors with his extraordinary, expressive shape. Kaffe's frog is based on a hand-coloured engraving of 1758 from Roesel Von Rosenhof's *Histoire Naturalis Ranarum*. In his book *Glorious Inspiration* Kaffe says how instructive these hand-coloured engravings can be. Their sharp, clear details are easily translated into other designs. Kaffe added his own lily pad, his own colouring and a watery green background for those who prefer to stitch the design as a rectangular-shaped cushion. It can be stitched either way – as a modelled cut-out or a flat cushion cover – and in the kit we provide the background wool so that the choice is yours.

Cut-outs are a very American idea, so it seems natural that Kaffe should have done a few. Too often they are cute but Kaffe makes his stylish. He stitched a lovely pair of ducks like this, in drifts of hazy colour, for his first book *Glorious Needlepoint* and returned to the theme recently with another pair in stronger tones. They allowed him to focus on the subtlety of shading found in ducks' feathers as the eye is not distracted with any background patterning. Here again the frog is a study in isolation and, I think, it illustrates how good Kaffe is with animals. He somehow catches their spirit in a way which is hard to explain. These cut-outs are humorous and fun, as well as being so well executed, and he even had plans once for stitching a life-size, cut-out cow. A distinctive feature of nearly all his work is its boldness. I have used that word before and it applies to his flowers or vegetables in the same way that it applies to his animals or shells. It reflects his personality. There are no half-measures with Kaffe. Whenever he stitches he stitches with conviction and as the years go by this characteristic becomes more emphatic.

When Kaffe Fassett first used an eight mesh rug canvas to stitch cushion covers (for his fruits in *Glorious Needlepoint*) there was a chorus of reproval from 'professional' needleworkers. The more experienced a needlework designer the finer the canvas. That had always been the accepted progression. This was based on a residual belief that needlework design was as much about technical expertise as artistic flair. For Kaffe to suddenly stride in the opposite direction was a startling move. He did so for two reasons: stitching on a wider gauge of canvas was quicker and more immediate. The pattern grew in front of your eyes making it more exciting. The other reason was one of technical, artistic skill. He was able, at this stage, to convey the subtleties of movement and tone on this wider gauge of canvas. There are very few designers who can. Only eleven colours are used in the 'Lily Pad Frog' and yet, worked in these bold stitches, he has the balance and delicacy of petit-point.

CANVAS: 8 holes to the inch

STITCH: Half-cross or tent

DESIGN AREA: 20in × 15in (51cm × 38cm)

YARN: Paternayan

Shade	Paternayan	
Black	221	3 skeins
Forest Green	601	4 skeins
Leaf Green	692	4 skeins
Leaf Green	693	4 skeins
Pale Spring Green	635	7 skeins
Pale Yellow	726	2 skeins
Pale Pink	935	2 skeins
Dark Brown	410	1 skein
Mid-brown	433	2 skeins
Lime Yellow	762	2 skeins
Peacock Blue	521	11 skeins

Chart overleaf.

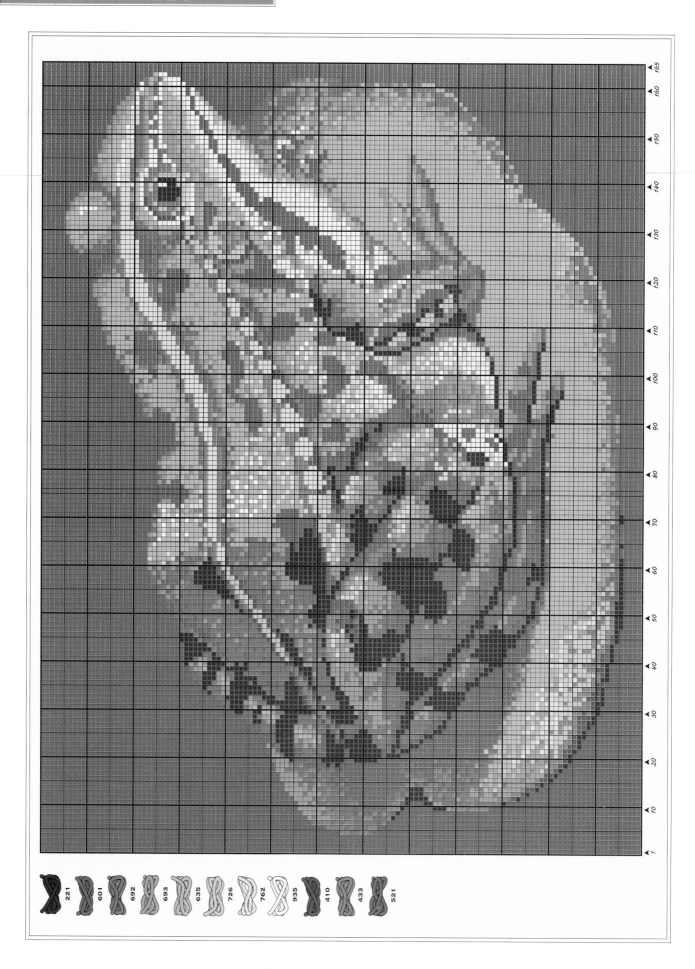

221 601 692 693 635 726 762 935 410 433 521

NOTES

Alison McDonnell's 'Notes' won joint first prize in a competition we ran at the Glasgow School of Art. Like many of the best things in life this came about by accident. I was having lunch with Patrick Gottelier who runs Artwork, the knitwear company. Barbara Santos-Shaw, the head of printed textiles at Glasgow, was visiting his studio that day with a group of her students. She suggested that we should put up a prize and run some sort of competition for her students to design a needlepoint kit. The idea admittedly had her backing but I was amazed how enthusiastically it was received by the students. It was open to any second-year student and nearly all took part. There were also requests from final year students to participate and a number of them did.

Ten years ago if I had offered a prize to textile students, at any art college, to design a needlepoint kit I would have been lucky to get one interested party. It would have been way beneath their dignity – too commercial and, in their eyes, frankly 'naff'. It illustrates the change in profile needlework has undergone. It also illustrates a changed attitude in artistic circles to the crafts generally. After the designer 1980s when everything down to a cigarette lighter was 'designed' the mood has changed. Students are now less interested in designing for mass production and the unique object is once again chic. The Conran Shop, in London –

always a good barometer in such matters – is currently full of mass-produced furniture trying to give the impression that each piece is different: a series of craftsman-made one-offs. The era of matt black, chrome and stainless steel is now over and with its passing the crafts have gained a new respectability.

I was impressed by the way Alison approached her task. She, like nearly all the other students, had never stitched or designed a needlepoint before. The brief allowed for artwork to be presented in whatever form the competitor felt most comfortable with. Alison decided that she needed to learn how to stitch to really understand the possibilities of this new medium, and did just that. She then proceeded to stitch this design, laboriously unpicking and reworking sections over and over again. Her painstaking attention to detail has paid off. The loose style of the cushion with its collaged composition is counterbalanced by the fine detail of the stitching (look at the notes in the border) and the subtle, sophisticated use of colour. She quickly realised that in almost any type of needlework design wools work-up best when shaded softly and the differing shades of brown stripe blend beautifully with the 1950s mustards, orange and blue. Here is an excellent example of why it is always worth trying something new and I hope we can organise similar competitions in the future.

OVERLEAF: A PRIZE-WINNING DESIGN FROM THE GLASGOW
SCHOOL OF ART WHERE WE RAN A COMPETITION TO ENCOURAGE
YOUNG DESIGNERS TO TRY OUT NEEDLEPOINT. MANY OF THE
OTHER SUBMISSIONS WERE EQUALLY EXCITING

The idea of employing notes and sheet music in needlework has more mileage to it. I like the way Alison McDonnell uses it for incorporation into her overall collage but there are many other possibilities. A simple and effective one is to stitch it straight. A piano stool of sheet music in charcoal grey and white was suggested by Jacqueline Coleman who runs our shop, and you could stitch a highly original cushion in the same way. Sheet music creates the most fascinating patterns. It is one of the few ways to stitch in two colours only without getting bored. A theme to explore perhaps?

CANVAS: 12 holes to the inch

STITCH: Half-cross or tent

DESIGN AREA: 20in × 20in (51cm × 51cm)

YARN: Anchor Tapisserie or Paternayan

Shade	Anchor	Paternayan	
Priest Grey	9768	221	7 skeins
Dusty Pink	8368	923	1 skein
Salmon Pink	8306	864	2 skeins
Rust Orange	8162	851	4 skeins
Flame Red	8196	821	1 skein
Dusty Pink	8366	923	1 skein
Sky Blue	8824	502	2 skeins
Sky Blue	8820	503	3 skeins
Cornflower Blue	8686	545	1 skein
Lime	9274	671	4 skeins
Heraldic Gold	9282	760	2 skeins
Old Gold	8012	263	1 skein
Cinnamon	9388	442	3 skeins
Cinnamon	9386	443	3 skeins
Khaki	9324	444	2 skeins
Rust Orange	8168	810	3 skeins
Cathedral Blue	8792	511	1 skein
Cream	8004	262	16 skeins

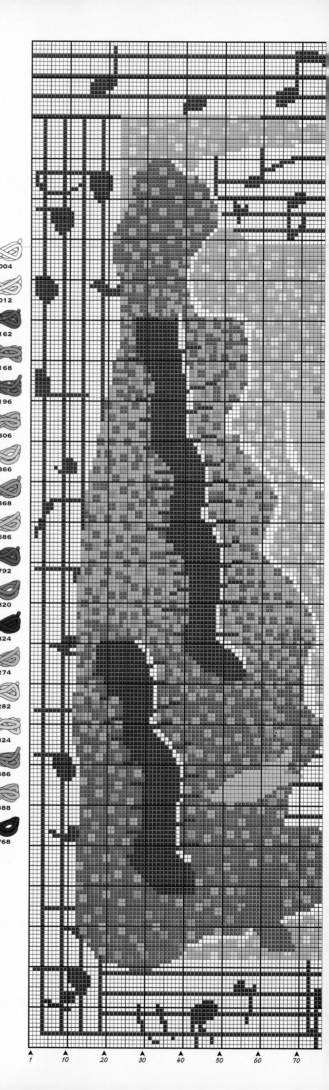

Chapter Five

OLD FLORALS

"Art weary? here's the place
For weariness to rest,
These flowers are herbs of grace
To cure the aching breast;
Soft beds these mossy banks
Where dewdrops only weep,
Where nature 'turns God thanks
And sings herself to sleep.
Art troubled with strife? Come hither
Here's peace and summer weather."

JOHN CLARE, 'COME HITHER'

ALPHABET CUSHION

Both of the last two chapters focused on the new. For this final chapter we have a group of designs which draw their inspiration from the past. Most of the designers we work with have a knowledge and appreciation of older textiles. Candace Bahouth, for example, is immersed in the medieval period while Jill Gordon and Margaret Murton are more interested in the seventeenth and eighteenth centuries. All the designs we will see in this chapter are based on textile patterns from the past, but they are not 'repro' – copies of old patterns stitched verbatim. When a contemporary designer travels back in time it is to re-examine the achievements of previous generations in order to create something new. All of these floral designs openly profess their origins but each is the personal work of an individual designer. The past is not aped with awed servility, it is explored. The wonderful colours and inventive ideas that crowd upon you when looking at textiles in a museum should act as a springboard for the imagination. Creative designers take ideas and inspiration from different eras. So if you are interested in needlework design where better to start than in a museum? Kaffe Fassett based a whole book on ideas that sparked his imagination when looking at objects in the Victoria and Albert Museum in London. If you are serious about needlework design you need to be acquainted with what has gone before. A sense of history provides an understanding of the present. Museums are not dusty, dull cathedrals of academe fit only for school parties. They are intoxicating visual libraries assembled over many, many years. Let's use them!

We start the chapter with a design that has perhaps the faintest historical link of any. Anita Gunnett's 'Alphabet Cushion' has a trelliswork pattern interspersed with spring flowers in pale, contemporary colours. There is nothing remotely 'historical' about that. But the use of a single central letter transcribed from an alphabetical chart does give this pattern a link with the past. It is reminiscent of samplers and the long needlework tradition of working individual letters and motifs for technical practice as much as for decorative effect. It is generally acknowledged that

the original function of an embroidered sampler was educational. It had a twofold purpose: as an experimental exercise in learning and practice, and as a record of stitch and pattern for the future.

The Elizabethan period was the second great era of English needlework and it coincided with an addiction for all things embroidered: bags, purses, collars, gloves, handkerchiefs, jackets, bodices, smocks, waistcoats, shirts, bookbindings, carpets for tables and covers, bed covers, cushions, hangings, shoes, you name it, it was embroidered. A wealth of sumptuous materials drenched in a plethora of stitches trumpeted rank and status. Stitching was required at all levels of society and at all levels of technical ability. The alphabet appeared so regularly in samplers because it provided practice for marking linen. Throughout the seventeenth and eighteenth centuries most girls between the ages of five and fifteen worked at least one during their schooldays. They were sometimes worked in silk and silver gilt threads and many new stitches were used. The late sixteenth and early seventeenth centuries saw the introduction of Algerian eye or star stitch, Hungarian, Gobelin, Florentine, rococo, long-armed cross and eyelet stitches.

Right up until the mid-nineteenth century the majority of working women were still employed in three distinct occupations: agriculture, domestic service and as 'needlewomen'. During the eighteenth century samplers became more pictorial depicting Biblical scenes and landscapes. They also illustrated changed attitudes in society. With the rise of methodism and the influence of Wesley samplers are found expressing pious thoughts with stitched selections from scripture devoid of decoration or embellishment. With the mechanisation of textile production in the nineteenth century society's requirements for embroidery and for skilled broderers diminished. This was reflected in the declining standard of samplers. Embroidery had become, at its higher end, a social grace, an exercise in concentration and dexterity, but it had lost the progressive vitality of earlier times. Now we stitch reproductions of historical samplers for no better reason than that we like the look of them.

A SIMPLE PATTERN WITH THE FEEL OF A SAMPLER.

WE THOUGHT IT A NICE CHANGE TO PRODUCE A KIT

WHICH COULD BE PERSONALISED

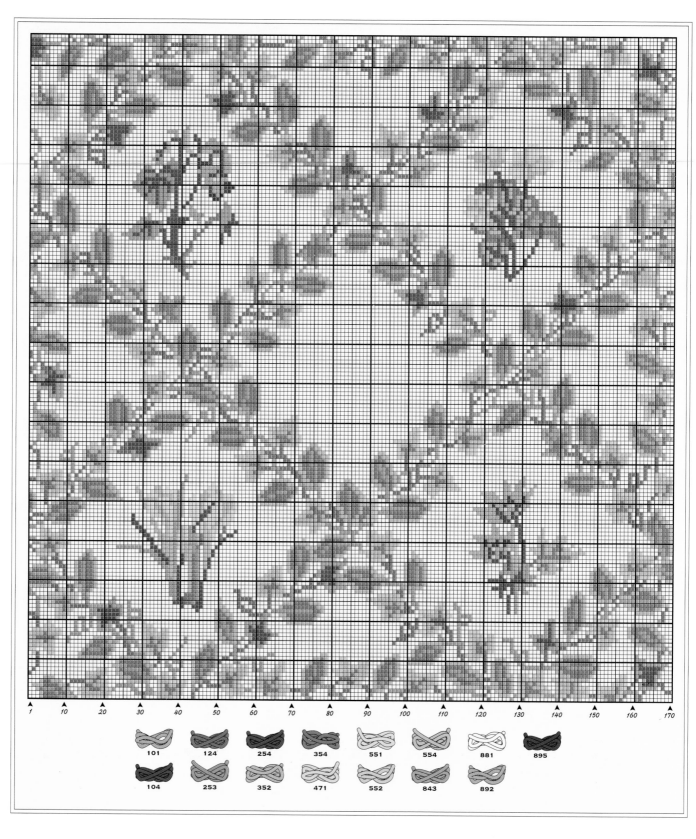

1   10   20   30   40   50   60   70   80   90   100   110   120   130   140   150   160   170

101   124   254   354   551   554   881   895

104   253   352   471   552   843   892

The idea of this pattern is to personalise it with an initial of your choice. The central panel is left empty for this purpose. The geometric structure of the design, however, would allow you to replace the individual spring flowers with other motifs should you wish. It could become in this way like so many samplers were in the past, a personal scrap book of familiar and favourite images. Many samplers from the seventeenth and eighteenth centuries, usually stitched by children, were a charming amalgam of animals, houses, trees, birds and insects mixed in with the lettering.

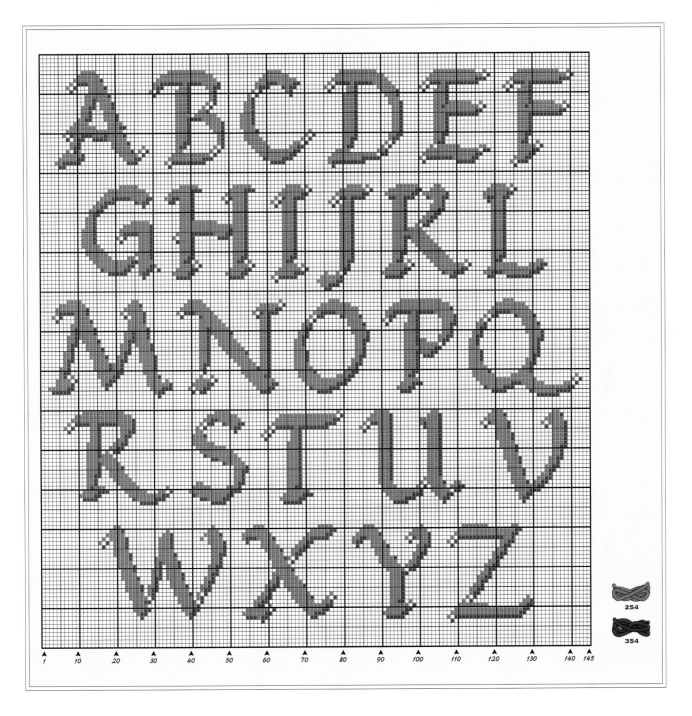

254

354

CANVAS: 12 holes to the inch

STITCH: Half-cross or tent

DESIGN AREA: 14in × 14in (36cm × 36cm)

YARN: Appleton Tapestry wool or Paternayan

Shade	Appleton	Paternayan	
Purple	101	313	1 skein
Purple	104	312	1 skein
Terracotta	124	484	2 skeins
Grass Green	253	693	3 skeins
Grass Green	254	692	2 skeins

Shade	Appleton	Paternayan	
Grey Green	352	605	4 skeins
Grey Green	354	603	4 skeins
Autumn Yellow	471	727	3 skeins
Bright Yellow	551	773	1 skein
Bright Yellow	552	713	1 skein
Bright Yellow	554	771	1 skein
Heraldic Gold	843	733	1 skein
Pastel White	881	262	18 skeins
Hyacinth	892	313	1 skein
Hyacinth	895	310	1 skein

CHALICE OF FRUITS

The seventeenth and eighteenth centuries were the centuries, above all others, that saw the commercial expansion of Europe. Huge wealth was accumulated by energetic, enterprising and determined men and this new merchant prosperity spread itself widely. The last vestiges of the medieval world, with its narrowly prescribed structures of power and patronage, were transformed into a broader economic pluralism. The foundations of our own world were laid: the creation of a European bourgeoisie, the emergence of the professions and the growing importance of money within the social hierarchy. In varying degrees this process happened across Europe and much of the new wealth found its way into country estates. Owning land became an important avenue to a rise in social rank and once you had some land you needed a fine house built on it which itself needed to be lavishly furnished.

The medieval lord had ruled by personal contact with his supporters. This meant travelling with his retinue from one great house to the next. Tapestries, folding beds and chairs, chests, embroidered cushions and hangings came along too. With the passing of this way of life a house became a more settled affair – a home. The interior furnishings were conceived along with the architecture of the building. Interiors were planned as static set-pieces. This gave scope for finer detail and the greater elaboration of furniture and furnishings in general. Architects and pattern books travelled extensively across Europe and a new classical style emerged which affected all aspects of a building. It was common for a French architect in the seventeenth century to insist on controlling every aspect of the interior – the application of the Renaissance ideals of unity.

With this greater emphasis on visual co-ordination we see recurrent motifs and decorative devices popping-up in an almost interchangeable manner. From what source would Neil McCallum have taken his stylised vase and fruits? It could have been a plasterwork frieze, a fabric pattern, a piece of furniture. It would be impossible to say. Floral sprays, garlanded repeats, classical urns, cartouches or armorial compositions are not associated with a particular

This design from Neil McCallum has a 'country house' flavour. What does this ubiquitous but vague term conjure up? As with so many useful, generalised and inclusive classifications it is difficult to be precise. In England we would probably think of Colefax and Fowler, the National Trust, Wellington boots and labradors. It has as much to do with a way of life as with a particular style. But in terms of architecture and furnishings it has a wider European dimension. In the seventeenth and eighteenth centuries buildings and their interiors across Europe developed along broadly similar lines with many features in common. It was a look which subsequently crossed the Atlantic too. The Palladian proportions of James Hoban's White House, the pillared facades of the plantation houses in the south, or the Georgian town architecture of Boston and New York look as familiar to a European as they do to an American.

product. They are associated with a period and Neil's cushion is at home there. Being such a universal style for so long, enduring designs like these blend in happily nowadays. From the mid seventeenth-century less time was spent in embroidering cushions. More attention was paid to their presentation with trimmings and fringes in prominence. From about 1630 it was common for many fine cushions to be finished-off with four large tassels, one at each corner, and we decided to do the same with 'Chalice of Fruits'.

SMART AND SEDATE, NEIL MCCALLUM (PICTURED OPPOSITE) OPTS FOR RICH COLOURS WITH THIS TRADITIONAL PATTERN. IT WORKS IN A GRAND SETTING OR THE RELATIVE SIMPLICITY CHOSEN HERE BY ZOE AND TIM HILL

This is a pattern for trying with different coloured backgrounds. Darker ones would look good: navy blue, a deep red or chocolate brown could all work well. As you can see from the list of shade numbers below Neil has gone to town on the detail. It would be possible to simplify a little if you wanted but it would be a shame. This design comes as close to the feel of a hand-painted canvas as a printed kit ever will. It is partly due to the choice of a twelve mesh canvas for what is quite a large cushion cover, but it is mainly due to the number of colours. So many colours enable a wealth of subtle shade changes normally associated with hand-painted canvases.

CANVAS: 12 holes to the inch

STITCH: Half-cross or tent

DESIGN AREA: 20in × 14in (51cm × 36cm)

YARN: Appleton Tapestry wool or Paternayan

Shade	Appleton	Paternayan	
Purple	103	312	1 skein
Terracotta	128	920	1 skein
Dull Rose Pink	144	912	2 skeins
Dull Rose Pink	145	911	2 skeins
Olive Green	243	642	3 skeins
Grass Green	253	693	2 skeins
Jacobean Green	295	601	2 skeins
Red Fawn	301	435	2 skeins
Brown Olive	315	D511	2 skeins
Cornflower	465	540	2 skeins
Autumn Yellow	471	727	2 skeins
Autumn Yellow	474	725	2 skeins
Autumn Yellow	475	723	1 skein
Autumn Yellow	476	722	1 skein
Early English Green	548	600	2 skeins
Paprika	721	872	1 skein
Rose Pink	757	902	2 skeins
Rose Pink	759	900	2 skeins
Biscuit Brown	765	412	2 skeins
Coral	863	862	1 skein
Pastel White	882	263	18 skeins
Pastel Lavender	883	D147	1 skein
Hyacinth	894	312	2 skeins
Golden Brown	903	442	1 skein
Fawn	916	450	2 skeins
Putty Grounding	985	463	2 skeins
Charcoal	998	221	1 skein

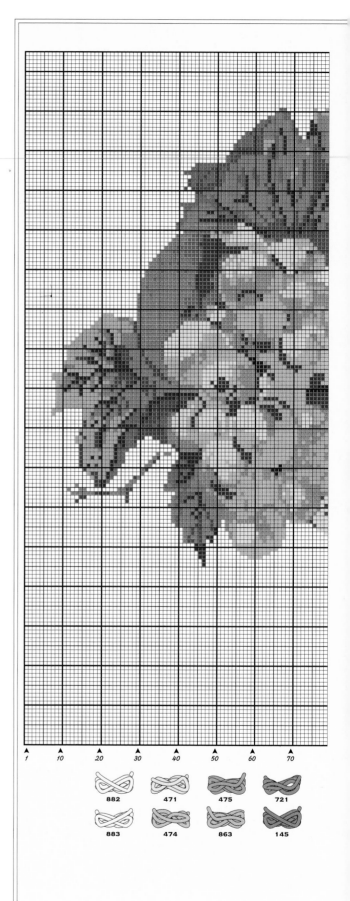

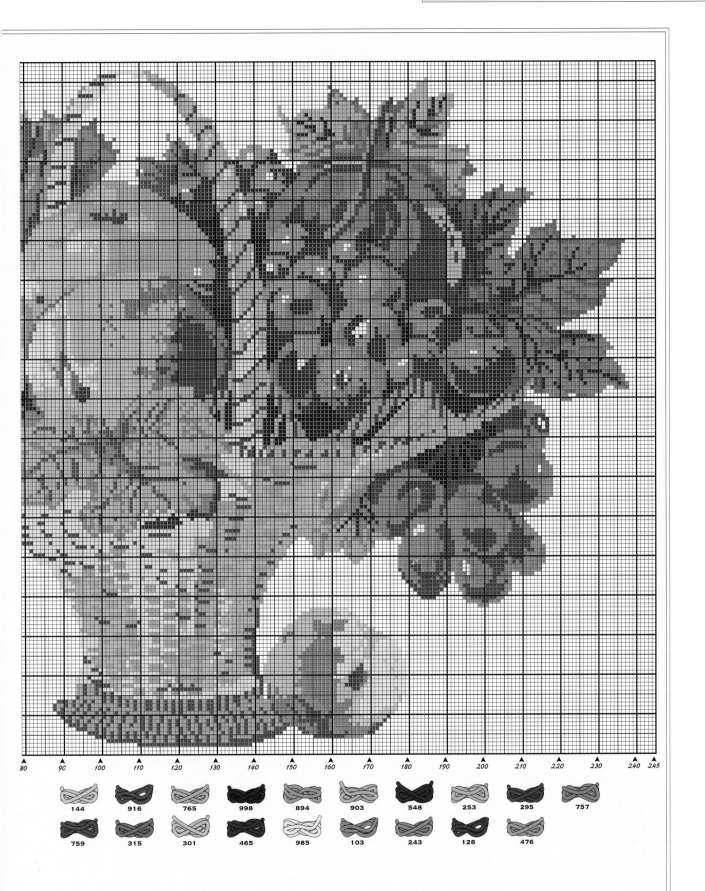

A MINI TRIO

There has been great demand recently for smaller kits to stitch. In general needlepoint kits have been getting larger, and not only ours. Designers usually like to work on a larger scale. It gives far greater scope for real design and, as a result, Ehrman have been producing more hangings and rugs than usual. But these larger kits do take a long time to stitch and they are expensive. They are also rather cumbersome and it was inevitable that there should, at some stage, be a reaction with people looking for simpler, quicker, cheaper projects which could fit easily into a bag for taking on holiday or to work on when travelling. Two years ago Glorafilia produced a series of four blue and white mini designs based on china patterns. They were different, fresh and appealing and I wasn't a bit surprised to hear how well they had sold. Word travels fast in the small world of the needlework trade and, always ready to cash in on a trend, here we are, a little later, with our own offering! I think Anita Gunnett has been wise to choose a fourteen mesh canvas for her designs. It allows for some detail. The charm of embroidery on a small scale lies in its detail. When you think of embroidered handkerchiefs, gloves or purses you think of the jewel-like quality of petit-point. Kaffe Fassett has some beautiful slippers in his new book also worked on fourteen mesh canvas. I think there is no escaping fine canvas for designs of this size and, anyway, it makes a pleasant change from the long-stitch or seven mesh rug canvas of our larger kits.

We first met Anita at the Royal School of Needlework. When we started our business our two principal designers were Kaffe Fassett and the Royal School of Needlework. It is hard to think of two more contrasting styles but that was partly the idea. We felt that we needed to balance Kaffe's innovative and modern design with a more traditional look if we were to appeal to a wide audience. We have always looked for good design wherever we can find it. The style is immaterial, what matters is the intrinsic quality of the work. The Royal School were sitting on a wealth of archive material including original designs for canvas work by Walter Crane and Burne-Jones. It was criminally underutilized and we commissioned their design department to produce a series of kits for us many of which drew on this rich seam of archive material. The Royal School has always been a curious hybrid of an institution. Their primary function has traditionally been textile conservation and restoration along with commissioned work, much of it ceremonial. At the same time they have sporadically produced their own commercial designs, either as painted canvases or as kits, but in a rather haphazard, unplanned fashion. This is a shame as they have an interesting store of patterns. This year they have started to market their own range of kits which is a serious attempt to do something about this. It may mean competition for the rest of us but it should be welcomed by needleworkers generally. If handled properly this time it will resurrect a fine collection of design which has been lying dormant for far too long. It should enhance the choice of kits available.

Anita was working in the Royal School's design department in the early 1980s and was responsible for a number of our kits. Another designer working there at the time was Susan Skeen. They both went free-lance and we have continued to work with them, on and off, ever since. It is very nice to have some new patterns from Anita and these small canvases could be used in a number of ways. They make attractive little pictures in their own right, almost like textile fragments, or they could be bordered to make small cushions. A group of them could be combined to make a larger patchwork or they could even be used for patching clothes. A German magazine ran a reader offer last year of Candace Bahouth's 'Cherubs'. I was astonished to see how they had used it. They had cut it into segments and patched a jean jacket with it. With a little imagination its remarkable what you can do with a piece of needlepoint.

THREE SMALLER CANVASES FROM ANITA GUNNETT: CHEAPER, QUICKER AND LESS BULKY. WE HAVE HAD AN INCREASING NUMBER OF REQUESTS FOR KITS OF THIS SIZE

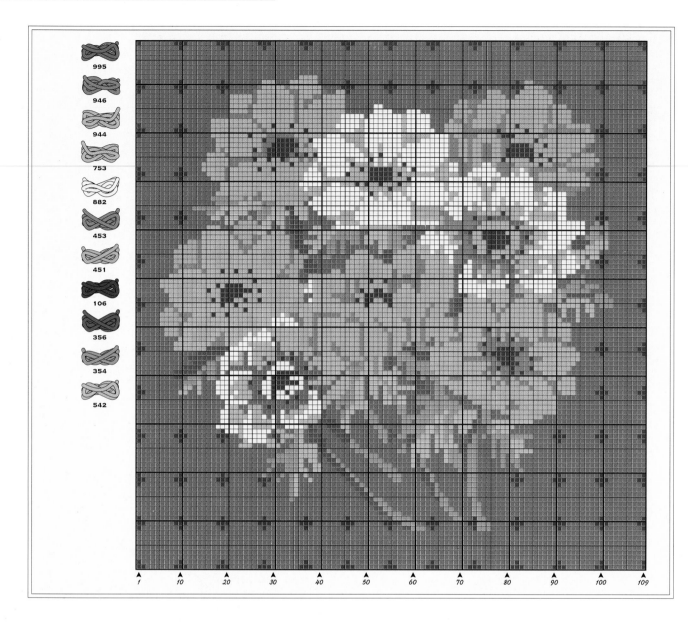

These three small designs could be worked up as bags. In her book, *Medieval Needlepoint*, Candace Bahouth produced a range of smaller designs, on finer canvas, for evening bags with metal thread and beads. This added sparkle. There are catalogues of beads available with a huge selection of colours and materials, and these beads can be quite simply overstitched.

ANEMONES SQUARE

CANVAS: 14 holes to the inch

STITCH: Half-cross or tent

DESIGN AREA: 8in × 8in (20cm × 20cm)

YARN: Appleton Tapestry wool or Paternayan

Shade	Appleton	Paternayan	
Cherry Red	995	940	6 skeins
Bright Rose Pink	946	903	1 skein
Bright Rose Pink	944	904	2 skeins
Rose Pink	753	D281	2 skeins
Pastel White	882	263	2 skeins
Mauve	453	302	1 skein
Mauve	451	323	1 skein
Purple	106	320	2 skeins
Grey Green	356	601	1 skein
Grey Green	354	603	3 skeins
Early English Green	542	653	1 skein

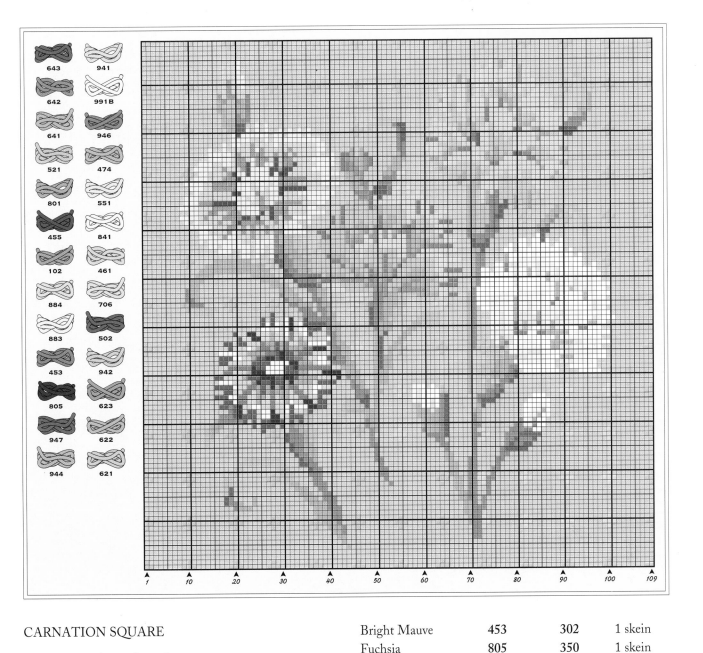

CARNATION SQUARE

CANVAS: 14 holes to the inch

STITCH: Half-cross or tent

DESIGN AREA: 8in × 8in (20cm × 20cm)

YARN: Appleton Tapestry wool or Paternayan

Shade	Appleton	Paternayan	
Peacock Blue	643	602	1 skein
Peacock Blue	642	D546	1 skein
Peacock Blue	641	523	1 skein
Turquoise	521	525	1 skein
Fuchsia	801	353	1 skein
Bright Mauve	455	301	1 skein
Purple	102	312	1 skein
Pastel Lilac	884	314	1 skein
Pastel Heather	883	D147	1 skein
Bright Mauve	453	302	1 skein
Fuchsia	805	350	1 skein
Bright Rose Pink	947	902	1 skein
Bright Rose Pink	944	904	1 skein
Bright Rose Pink	941	934	1 skein
Bright White	991B	260	1 skein
Bright Rose Pink	946	903	1 skein
Autumn Yellow	474	725	1 skein
Bright Yellow	551	773	1 skein
Heraldic Gold	841	704	1 skein
Cornflower	461	564	8 skeins
Flesh Tint	706	492	2 skeins
Scarlet	502	841	1 skein
Bright Rose Pink	942	933	1 skein
Flamingo	623	833	1 skein
Flamingo	622	834	1 skein
Flamingo	621	835	1 skein

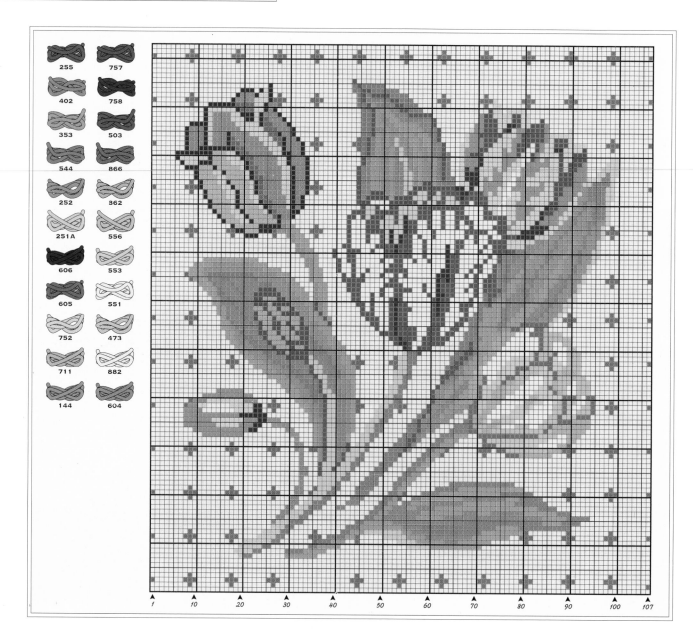

TULIP SQUARE

CANVAS: 14 holes to the inch

STITCH: Half-cross or tent

DESIGN AREA: 8in × 8in (20cm × 20cm)

YARN: Appleton Tapestry wool or Paternayan

Shade	Appleton	Paternayan	
Grass Green	255	651	1 skein
Sea Green	402	612	1 skein
Grey Green	353	604	1 skein
Early English Green	544	692	1 skein
Grass Green	252	694	1 skein
Grass Green	251A	653	1 skein
Mauve	606	310	1 skein

Shade	Appleton	Paternayan	
Mauve	605	311	1 skein
Rose Pink	752	945	1 skein
Wine Red	711	914	1 skein
Dull Rose Pink	144	912	1 skein
Rose Pink	757	902	1 skein
Rose Pink	758	901	1 skein
Scarlet	503	951	1 skein
Coral	866	850	1 skein
Coral	862	854	1 skein
Bright Yellow	556	813	1 skein
Bright Yellow	553	772	1 skein
Bright Yellow	551	773	1 skein
Autumn Yellow	473	732	1 skein
Pastel White	882	263	7 skeins
Mauve	604	312	1 skein

SAVONNERIE

Jill Gordon called this design 'Savonnèrie' for its colour rather than its composition. The designs of the Savonnèrie tended to be grand and formal in contrast to the more domestic patterns of Aubusson. The name Savonnèrie came from the original building housing production which was a former soap factory. Every month a painter from the Royal Academy inspected designs and gave drawing lessons for the design staff. With the explosion of royal building taking place the Savonnèrie's production was reserved for the crown. In addition to all the work undertaken for the Louvre, in 1682 the court was installed at Versailles and that too needed filling. During this period all design was supervised by Charles Lebrun and it was intended to reflect the glories of the age. A uniform style had emerged with garlands of flowers and bold leafscrolls set against black or brown backgrounds. The practice of having an artist in charge of design continued throughout the eighteenth century with Lebrun being succeeded by Belin de Fontenay in 1667. He had been a flower painter at the Gobelins and brought with him a lighter touch. By the middle of the eighteenth century rococo devices were appearing: palm trees, shells, bat wings and fleur-de-lys; and also lighter colours. Pink, yellow, pale blue, and white replaced the earlier black and deep brown backgrounds. Jill's colours are nearer to this period of the Savonnèrie's production.

THE EHRMAN NEEDLEPOINT BOOK

Jill's colours are beautifully soft. They succeed in looking like the bleached colours of old textiles where the passage of time and the effects of the sun have taken their toll. They are brought into relief, just when they might have merged themselves away into a vapour, with the crisp blue of a summer sky. Far too often backgrounds are a single, flat colour. Just look what the patterned background adds to this design. It puts it in a different league adding depth and perspective. Jill Gordon, like so many of our designers, started life as a painter. The slightly off-centred combination of fruits and flowers, the muted drifts of attenuated colour and the mottled blues of the sky all remind me of her watercolours and give this pattern its relaxed, easy air.

CANVAS: 10 holes to the inch

STITCH: Half-cross or tent

DESIGN AREA: 16in × 16in (41cm × 41cm)

YARN: Appleton Tapestry wool or Paternayan

Shade	Appleton	Paternayan	
Dull Rose Pink	141	924	3 skeins
Flame Red	205	872	3 skeins
Drab Green	332	643	6 skeins
Drab Green	334	642	4 skeins
Drab Green	341	644	2 skeins
Honeysuckle Yellow	692	754	6 skeins
Honeysuckle Yellow	693	734	5 skeins
Bright China Blue	743	561	3 skeins
Bright China Blue	746	560	3 skeins
Rose Pink	754	913	3 skeins
Rose Pink	757	902	2 skeins
Biscuit Brown	766	D419	3 skeins
Pastel White	882	263	4 skeins
Pastel Blue	886	564	2 skeins
Golden Brown	902	442	6 skeins

This design really does manage to capture the faded feel of an older fabric. As a result it could be used in a number of ways. Sections of woven tapestries are sometimes used to cover folders or binders and 'Savonnèrie' would be a good design for that. It would make a lovely needlepoint bag or stool top and would go well on a round footstool. Starting at the centre of the chart simply mark off the area you would need to stitch depending on the measurements of your footstool. Although you will cut into the design it doesn't matter. As the design is based on fabric patterns it can be used, like a fabric, for all sorts of upholstery.

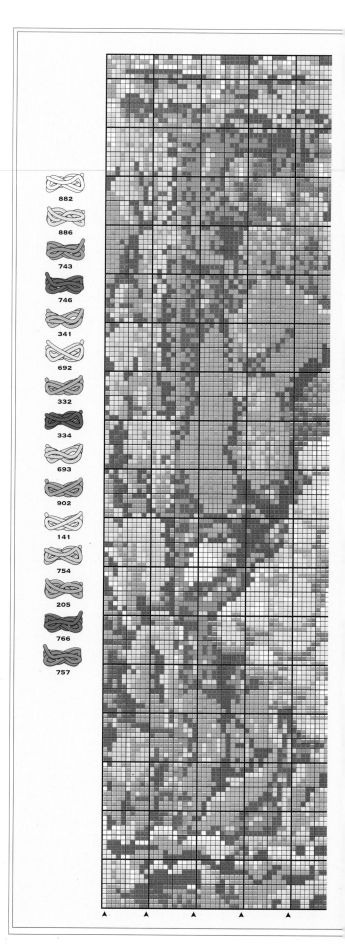

SUMMER

Margaret Murton's Tardis has taken her back to the late sixteenth century. In the tapestries of Brussels and Mortlake a notable feature of these hangings were their borders. Garlanded festoons of flowers and vegetables struggle for space with tumbling cascades of fruit. Wheat sheaves and the gifts of mother nature compete with swagged cornucopias for any available toe-hold. These borders are literally overflowing with natural produce and initially the eye is submerged under a tidal wave of detail. But then they are only borders and were never intended to be viewed as independent designs. They are sumptuous sources of inspiration and when people talk of the 'richness of tapestry' I often think of these fecund riots.

The way Margaret Murton works illustrates how a contemporary designer uses the past. As a watercolourist she began painting decorative florals and fruits on old wooden panels for houses in France and England. They are lovely, the wood enhancing her faded, washed use of paint. It is always a joy to receive her artwork which normally comes as a watercolour painting. Margaret lives in Leicestershire in a very attractive and still relatively unspoilt part of the country. She works from the nature that surrounds her. Her sketchbook brims with fields of daisies, honeysuckle tendrils twining through briar roses, studies of leaves and fruits, berries and plants. These are the elements which are arranged and rearranged into her designs. As she herself says her floral and fruit motifs are 'found in almost all Flemish and French tapestries of the sixteenth and seventeenth centuries', but hers are her own. It is what I meant at the beginning of the chapter when I said that a contemporary designer travels back in time to re-examine the achievements of previous generations in order to create something new. The context is there, the colours are there – subdued creams, dusty golds and pinks, Prussian and indigo blues – but the design, the actual composition, is quite new. These designs are not copies of old borders. Old borders act as the springboard for Margaret's imagination. And the same goes for all the designs in this chapter. Not one of them is a copy of an existing historical piece. They are all the original works of living artists.

Margaret would be the first to admit how difficult it then is to reduce the infinite variations of paint into a selected band of roughly twenty colours. If you start from a watercolour painting, choosing your thread colours is the next process, and it is an art in itself. Whereas Kaffe Fassett or Elian McCready stitch their colour compositions as they go, Margaret works the other way around. Her challenge is to capture the colour essence of her original in wool. First

of all the design has to be graphed into the small squares which will correspond with the reticulated nature of the canvas (I always liked Hardy Amies's description of canvas embroidery as 'filling holes with wool'). This is like trying to splinter a raindrop. The only way to start is to place a sheet of graph paper over the painting and decide what are the predominant shades in each square. We only allow our designers a maximum of twenty-five colours and we get tetchy if they use that many! The preferred amount is anywhere between ten and twenty. The reason is purely eco-

DESIGNED TO LOOK LIKE A SECTION TAKEN FROM THE BORDER OF A SEVENTEENTH-CENTURY EUROPEAN WOVEN HANGING, MARGARET MURTON HAS ADDED A TOUCH OF HER OWN LIGHTER COLOUR TO SOFTEN THINGS A BIT

nomic. The cost of production rises disproportionately once you get over that sort of level. So the colour in each square has to be chosen from a very restricted menu. This process

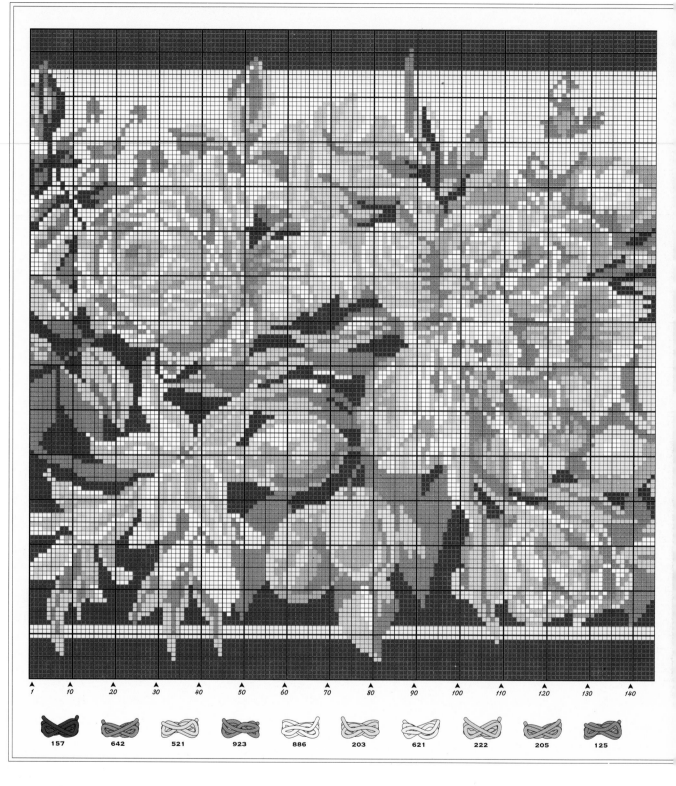

| 1 | 10 | 20 | 30 | 40 | 50 | 60 | 70 | 80 | 90 | 100 | 110 | 120 | 130 | 140 |

| 157 | 642 | 521 | 923 | 886 | 203 | 621 | 222 | 205 | 125 |

then goes back and forth. Working within your maximum prescribed total you may find halfway through for example that you are going to need two or three more greens. This will mean sacrificing a couple of blues and one of those pinks which, at a pinch, you could just live without. That means redesigning the section you had just completed to accord with the new palette. It is a skill and it is all a matter

of balance, judgement and compromise. Finally the actual selection of the wools takes place. Here the designer will be deciding on ten or twenty shades from a range of over three hundred. These need to recapture the original feel of the watercolour as closely as possible but they also need to work comfortably together when stitched. At this point some experimental stitching of different sections takes place until

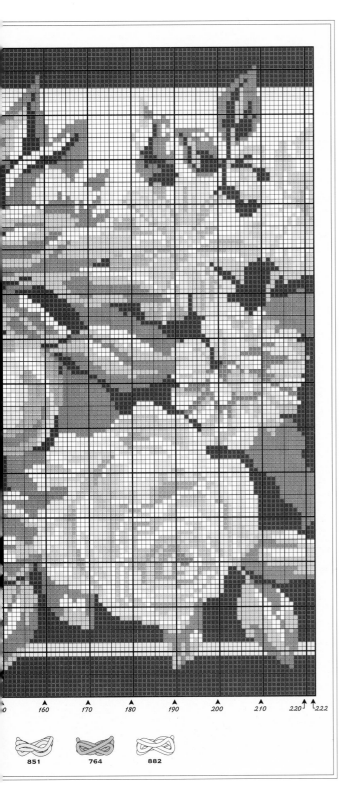

160   170   180   190   200   210   220 222

851   764   882

It is easy to see why designers like to work with fewer colour restrictions. The subtlety and beauty that can be achieved with fifty colours as opposed to twenty is immeasurably greater. This is one of the frustrations of producing printed canvases. I am always delighted when I hear that one of our designers has won a private commission. I know that with no restriction on colour he or she will, in all probability, produce something really interesting. If you are planning to stitch your own design, and particularly if you start with a watercolour, I would advise you to let rip on colour. Each hole has to be 'filled with wool' so why not make as many of them as different as possible. I am sure you will find the shading of flowers or fruits a lot easier with a good range of colours and once you get used to using a lot of colour it will seem quite natural. What is unnatural is our meanness with colour. Unfortunately, to produce a needlepoint kit, it has to be so; but, therein lies the skill of our designers.

CANVAS: 12 holes to the inch

STITCH: Half-cross or tent

DESIGN AREA: 18in × 12in (46cm × 30cm)

YARN: Appleton Tapestry wool or Paternayan

Shade	Appleton	Paternayan	
Terracotta	125	482	1 skein
Mid Blue	157	531	6 skeins
Flame Red	203	486	2 skeins
Flame Red	205	872	2 skeins
Bright Terracotta	222	933	2 skeins
Turquoise	521	525	3 skeins
Flamingo	621	835	2 skeins
Peacock Blue	642	D546	4 skeins
Biscuit Brown	764	413	2 skeins
Custard Yellow	851	D541	2 skeins
Pastel White	882	263	6 skeins
Pastel Blue	886	564	2 skeins
Dull China Blue	923	513	2 skeins

'Summer' is part of Margaret Murton's 'Four Seasons' series. 'Spring' was the most popular but I always preferred 'Summer' and 'Autumn'. Their colours are softer and Margaret is best when her colours merge and blend.

This pattern could almost be repeated, end to end, to produce a long runner or bell-pull to hang on a wall. It would need a little creative adaptation but it could be made to work.

the final formula is arrived at. There is a lot more to it than most people imagine: the whole design can be spoilt at the end if the wools stitch up darker or lighter than expected. It is impossible to pick your colours simply by looking at a shade card. The colours need to be worked-up to test relative densities and to iron out any unexpected surprises when two colours meet side-by-side.

129

OLD FLORALS

BLOOMING ROSES

Like the 'Berlin Roses' in the first chapter David Merry has adapted this pattern from mid-nineteenth century charts. This design, however, has a softer feel to it with a greater sense of motion and we toned the colours down further to match the mood. On the original Berlin Woolwork chart over fifty colours were used so the process of thinning them out was a painstaking business. To get this right you can't cut corners and if you are doing this yourself you will need to work-up sections to test how your colours react together.

Many shops, particularly in America, sell hand-painted canvases and wools separately. For those with a good eye and a little self-confidence it is a chance to select and combine their own colours. But the majority of stitchers do not have this self-confidence. When picking the shades of yarn for their hand-painted canvas most people rely on the advice of the shop owner. It was Candace Bahouth who pointed this out to me. It seemed shocking to her how casually these colours get chosen – reds, yellows, green or blues plucked almost at random to match the painted colour squares on the canvas. None of these colour combinations are tested and it is bound to be a hit and miss affair. A shopkeeper may, or may not, have a good eye for this sort of thing. A kit offers little flexibility, the quality of a printed canvas is undoubtedly inferior to that of a painted canvas, but at least you know that the colours will work-up as expected. When you buy a kit you buy the hours of agonizing and experimentation that lie behind the designers' final choice of yarns.

CANVAS: 12 holes to the inch

STITCH: Half-cross or tent

DESIGN AREA: 14in × 12in (36cm × 30cm)

YARN: Appleton Tapestry wool or Paternayan

Shade	Appleton	Paternayan	
White	991	261	1 skein
Flame Red	202	406	2 skeins
Flame Red	203	486	1 skein
Terracotta	124	484	2 skeins
Rose Pink	752	945	1 skein
Rose Pink	754	913	2 skeins
Bright Terracotta	225	931	2 skeins
Scarlet	504	950	3 skeins
Terracotta	128	920	2 skeins
Golden Brown	901	443	1 skein
Chocolate	182	463	1 skein
Red Fawn	302	412	1 skein
Chocolate	185	431	1 skein

	991		124		225		901		185		293		242		342		881

	202		752		504		182		401		647		345		333		998

	203		754		128		302		642		641		832		335

Sea Green	401	613	2 skeins		Bright Peacock Green	832	662	2 skeins
Peacock Green	642	D546	1 skein		Mid Olive Green	342	643	2 skeins
Jacobean Green	293	603	2 skeins		Drab Green	333	643	2 skeins
Peacock Green	647	660	1 skein		Drab Green	335	D511	2 skeins
Peacock Green	641	523	1 skein		*Background (choose one colour)*			
Olive Green	242	652	2 skeins		Pastel White	881	262	10 skeins
Mid Olive Green	345	642	1 skein		Charcoal	998	221	10 skeins

AUBUSSON

A
nd so we reach the final design in this book which comes from Candace Bahouth. Her Aubusson roses pattern works as a chairseat or cushion cover. The colours, although derived from the subdued, chalky tones of the eighteenth-century carpets, have a distinctive sparkle of their own. The little touches of lilac and pale green, along with the powder blues, add a freshness to this traditional design.

When looking at Jill Gordon's 'Savonnèrie' I mentioned Aubusson carpets. The designs of the Savonnèrie, destined as they were for the royal palaces of France, had a grandeur unsuited to most domestic interiors. Emblems, crests and weapons for the nobility set the tone for many Savonnèrie hangings whereas Aubusson carpets tended to feature a central motif surrounded by garlands or scatterings of flowers. Ribbons and bunches of flowers decorated plain, simple coloured backgrounds which were usually white, pale yellow or crimson. Most of these crimson backgrounds have now faded to crushed strawberry. If you think of Aubusson carpets you think of light, summery colours.

Aubusson carpets differed in style from the grander Savonnèrie weavings more from necessity than choice. They were cheaper. To be cheaper they had to use fewer colours and a bolder, less detailed, configuration of pattern; a less showy style of design developed largely as a result of cost restrictions. The painter Louis-Joseph Le Lorrain created a real innovation in design with his model 'à la grande mosaïque' in 1753, praised for its simplicity which did not distract the eye from the furniture in the room. Although Louis XV ordered carpets for the château at Choisy, and Napoleon commissioned pile carpets for Versailles and the

OLD FLORALS

CANDACE BAHOUTH SHOWS AN INSTINCTIVE FEEL FOR
THE POWDERY, CRUSHED COLOURS OF AUBUSSON CARPETS. THIS
CHAIRSEAT IS A ROMANTIC DESIGN OF SOFT EDGES AND BLURRED
FOCUS. 'BLOOMING ROSES' BY DAVID MERRY (PAGE 130–131)
WOULD FIT IN WELL ANYWHERE

Petit Trianon, most of the factory's output supplied the needs of France's growing bourgeoisie. Aubusson carpets regularly come up for sale at auction and if they are in reasonable condition will cost between £10,000 and £20,000. They have remained consistently popular because they are so easy to live with.

CANVAS: 10 holes to the inch

STITCH: Half-cross or tent

DESIGN AREA: 20in × 20in (51cm × 51cm)

YARN: Appleton Tapestry wool or Paternayan

Shade	Appleton	Paternayan	
Terracotta	125	482	2 skeins
Mid Blue	151	203	3 skeins
Mid Blue	152	514	3 skeins
Bright Terracotta	225	931	2 skeins
Olive Green	242	652	2 skeins
Dull Maine Blue	322	513	3 skeins
Mid Olive Green	343	643	2 skeins
Autumn Yellow	471	727	2 skeins
Early English Grass Green	542	653	2 skeins
Mauve	601	325	1 skein
Mauve	603	323	1 skein
Peacock Blue	646	661	1 skein
Honeysuckle Yellow	695	732	1 skein
Flesh Tint	706	492	2 skeins
Rose Pink	753	D281	2 skeins
Rose Pink	755	D275	2 skeins
Custard Yellow	851	D541	9 skeins
Bright Peacock Blue	853	511	2 skeins
Pastel White	881	262	3 skeins

This pattern was always envisaged by Candace as being a cushion as well as a chairseat. We have photographed it as a chairseat because we don't have any others in this book, but it would work just as well stitched as a cushion. Your chair will need to be the right shape for this pattern. It would spoil the design if you lost some of the ribbon border; so measure-up carefully before you start. As a cushion the surrounding ribbon border finishes the design off well. The soft colours would go with a wide variety of furnishings and being 20in (51cm) square it is a comfortable, but manageable, size.

THE EHRMAN NEEDLEPOINT BOOK

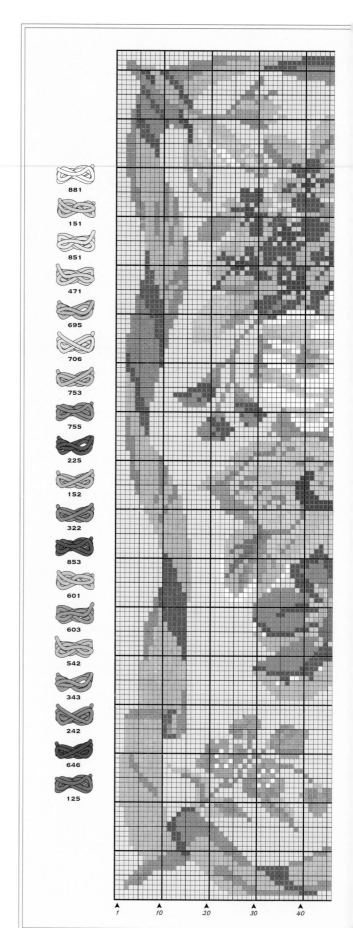

50   60   70   80   90   100   110   120   130   140   150   160   170   176

TECHNIQUES

Every design in this book can be easily stitched if you have the will and determination to do so. Once you have mastered the basic stitch it is simply a matter of repeating it and covering your canvas. The challenge with all these designs is in the shading, where a phenomenal spectrum of tone and colour has been used. Using a limited palette of colours, mixing and blending – as opposed to using hard blocks of colour – the designers have created these glorious patterns. Designing like this can be a fiddly business, but it is also true to say that many Ehrman customers welcome the opportunity to tackle something a bit more challenging. Until the mid 1980s all needlepoint kits were consciously designed for colour block printing. With the publication of Kaffe Fassett's *Glorious Needlepoint* in 1987 we embarked (rather fearfully) on more ambitious kit designs where shading played a greater part. We were always aware of the potential problems involved but, on balance, it has been well worthwhile. With such complex shading it is essential that only one stitch is used. We have always kept our kits restricted to half-cross or tent stitch for this very reason. The complexity is in the colour and to add different stitches to these detailed areas of pattern would be impractical. Different stitches add a textural dimension to a design but in our kits it is a luxury we must forego. If you are working one of our kits our advice would be to stick to the same stitch for anything other than a geometric border or other large area of single colour.

After many hours of hard work and hopefully enjoyment, you have a piece of stitched fabric. Once your design is completed there is no right or wrong way to finish it. Although once you have put all your time and effort into stitching it is worthwhile to finish your work in the best and most appropriate way possible. Many of the projects in this book have been made into cushions, but would work equally as well as hangings, chair covers, pictures or, by repeating the designs, as rugs. Remember also that by stitching on canvas you are crafting a new fabric. From the coarse canvas, a soft, strong, textured fabric appears and this can be used to make practical, yet decorative bags and clothing. Do not be inhibited by what you see, needlepoint has many potentials. What you decide to do with your work can be as creative as the needlepoint itself.

EQUIPMENT

FABRICS

All of the projects in this book are worked on canvas. Originally derived from hemp, it is a coarse yet versatile medium which is ideal for needlepoint. Nowadays you will find linen canvases, cotton and some synthetic ones. The cotton canvases are easiest to work with as they both handle and wash well. Synthetic canvas tends not to be suitable for making soft furnishings as it is made from a lightweight plastic which retains its stiffness once stitched; it is often used for three-dimensional projects.

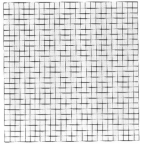
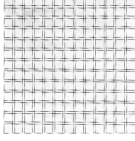

SINGLE THREAD   DOUBLE THREAD

The canvas is woven either with an evenweave single- or double-thread. The former is more common, but is prone to distort when handled, unless the canvas is mounted on a frame, and the finished piece blocked (see page 139). The double-thread canvas is stronger, consisting of pairs of threads woven together. This weave can be split allowing you to work half stitches and create fine detail.

The difference between canvases is determined by the number of holes per inch. The greater the number of holes per inch the finer the design. The size is referred to as the 'gauge' or 'mesh'. A large count can be fiddly to work and the design may take longer to grow than it would if you were working on a smaller gauge. The most frequently used canvases for working with a tapestry wool are between 10 and 16 holes to the inch. When working with rug wool or a thicker, coarser thread a smaller gauge canvas, 7 or even 5 holes per inch, is used. In such a case it is advisable to use a thicker thread as a normal four-ply tapestry wool may not cover the canvas.

You can work the same design on all gauges and you will find that the size of your finished project will differ depending on which size canvas you use.

THREADS

The projects in this book have been worked in tapestry yarns. A tapestry yarn is generally 100% wool. It does not stretch like a knitting yarn and is eminently stronger and more hard-wearing. The main brands used are Paternayan, also called Paterna, and Appletons and a DMC thread conversion chart is provided on page 142. Paternayan tapestry wool is four ply. You can split the strands to work in one, two, three or four strands as the pattern suggests. On a 14-gauge canvas you would expect to work with a single strand. Some of the designs use blended threads. To blend threads take one strand of each colour, thread them together through your needle and work with both strands. The effect is textured and very subtle.

You can work out the amount of thread you will need by measuring off a length of tapestry yarn and working a test section of your canvas until you run out of thread. Count the number of stitches and subtract 20%, i.e. if you work 40 stitches with a single strand 15in (38cm) piece of thread minus 20% of 40 stitches gives you 32 stitches. Then multiply this by the number of strands in the yarn, i.e. a four ply will give you four strands, so multiply 32 by four. This is the number of stitches you will be able to make with a 15in (38cm) length of thread, i.e. 128 stitches. The 20% gives a leeway for mistakes and for starting and finishing a length. You can work out how many stitches you will need in each colour by counting the blocks on the chart.

The 'how to' section of each project specifies how much of each colour you will need to work the projects on the gauge suggested. However you can use the method described above to calculate the amount of thread required if you want to work on a finer or a coarser gauge canvas, or if you choose to use a yarn other than the ones suggested.

NEEDLES

Needles used for needlepoint are blunt with a large eye. The blunt end slips easily through the holes in the canvas and the yarn can be threaded easily through the eye. A size 18 needle is correct for working a medium gauge canvas (10-14 holes per inch). Needles come in various different sizes which are suitable for the differing gauges of canvas which are available. As with canvas the higher the number the finer the needle.

GETTING STARTED

FOLLOWING A CHART

In order to stitch the designs in this book you will need to familiarise yourself with working from a chart. The charts are printed in full colour with the key running by the side. The key gives the appropriate thread numbers required for the project and each of these numbers are shown with a colour block which corresponds with the colours on the chart. Each of the coloured squares on the chart represents a single stitch.

Before you start make sure you have all the coloured yarns needed to work the design, you will need to sort them onto an organiser or mark them with bits of paper so you know which colour is which. It is also helpful to cut the skeins into manageable lengths. 15in (38cm) strands are convenient to work with.

PREPARING THE CANVAS

When cutting the canvas make sure it is at least 2in (5cm) larger all round than the finished design area specified 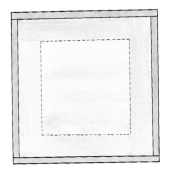 on the key. Bind the edges with masking tape to protect them from fraying. Lay the canvas on a piece of strong paper or card (blotting paper is ideal) and draw around the outline of the canvas. While you stitch your work may become distorted, but you can use this drawing of the original shape as a guide to block your work when you have finished stitching.

Find the centre of your canvas by folding it in half and then in quarters. Mark the point where the folds meet with a pencil or a couple of tacking (basting) stitches. This will be your starting point. It is easier to count the stitches from the chart if you work from the centre.

MOUNTING THE CANVAS ONTO A FRAME

You can work without a frame, however, it is not advisable because when working over your lap you are bound to stretch and distort your work more than necessary. By fixing your work to a frame you have a firm surface and the design will be easier to stitch.

There are several types of frame from which to choose. These include an adjustable roller frame, a stretcher frame or a tubular frame. Frames can be costly but are a very worthwhile investment as they will make stitching so much

STRETCHER FRAME

easier, and produce better final results. Ask at your local needlework shop for advice about the different types of frame that are available.

The least expensive and most basic, yet practical, is the stretcher frame. Interlocking lengths of wood form the frame. You will need two side pieces and a top and bottom the required length and width of your canvas. The canvas is then stretched and tacked to the frame. To do this mark the centre of each side of the frame and of each side of the canvas. Tack the canvas to the frame making sure to match up the centre marks on each side exactly. Make sure the canvas is pulled taut. As you tack the canvas in place keep the tacks symmetrical on each side of the frame to avoid distorting the material.

STITCHES

All the designs in this book use either tent stitch or half cross stitch. They are easy to work and grow quickly. It is a matter of personal choice which stitch you choose to work as they both look the same from the front. The half-cross stitch covers the horizontal on the back of the canvas and the tent stitch covers the vertical.

When stitching work all rows in the same direction to ensure a uniform appearance to the finished piece. Don't forget that if you turn your work around for any reason you should check your stitches still lie in the correct direction. Try to maintain an even stitch tension throughout.

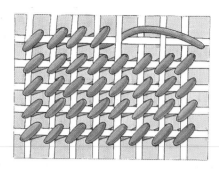

TENT STITCH

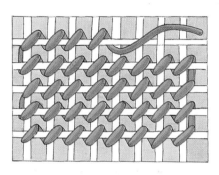

HALF CROSS STITCH

BEGINNING TO STITCH

Thread your needle and make a knot at the end of your thread. Starting a few canvas holes ahead of where you want to make your first stitch, take the needle down through the canvas to the wrong side, leaving the knot hanging on the right side. Bring it back up at the point of your first stitch and start stitching towards the knot. When you reach the knot cut it off.

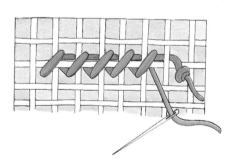

When you finish a length of yarn take the needle through two or three of the stitches at the back of the work, and then neatly trim the yarn close to the stitches to make a clean and tidy finish.

If your thread becomes tangled while you are stitching simply let go of the needle, letting it hang from your work. The thread should then twist and allow the tangle to unravel naturally.

FINISHING AND MAKING-UP

BLOCKING

When you have finished stitching the work should be blocked (or stretched) before being made into the finished article. This will bring back the original shape which may have been lost during stitching. First remove your work from the frame. Hold it up to the light to check that there are no missing stitches. Take your original card or blotting paper outline of the canvas and fix it with masking tape to a plywood board that is at least 2in (5cm) larger all around. Dampen the back of the worked canvas and place on top of the card or blotting paper wrong side up. Matching the corner of the canvas to the drawn guide, fix the work to the original drawing by gently pulling the canvas back into shape and keeping it in position with tacks hammered in place about 1in (2.5cm) apart. Allow this to dry naturally before removing. Badly distorted canvas might need stretching more than once.

WASHING

To wash your work use a mild detergent and lukewarm water. Do not rub or wring. If you do you may find the fibres will matt and start to felt. Be gentle and continue dipping until the water runs clear. Dry your work flat. If you are in any doubt about washing your needlework, always seek the advice of a dry cleaning specialist. This is particularly true of items of clothing such as the shells waistcoat on page 45.

CUSHION

On average the cushion size for the projects is 14in (35.5cm) square. However some are 16 and 18in (40.5 and 45.75cm). In view of this the following instructions are universal to cover all cushion sizes.

To make a simple cushion trim the edges of the canvas to leave a ⅝in (1.5cm) seam allowance around the stitched design. Place the worked canvas and piece of backing fabric, cut to the same size, together with right sides facing. Stitch around three sides and part of the fourth allowing a large enough gap to insert a cushion pad. If you buy a slightly bigger pad than the size of the cushion and squeeze it inside the cover it will give a plush full effect. A feather or down pad will produce a softer and more luxurious cushion – well worth the expense after all your hard work stitching. Turn the cushion cover right side out and slip stitch the edges of the canvas together.

INSERTING A ZIP FASTENER

To make a removable cushion cover, for cleaning, insert a zip into the cushion. Cut the edges off your canvas leaving a ⅝in (1.5cm) allowance around your design. Cut the backing fabric, the same width as your canvas but 1¼in (3cm) longer. Cut the backing fabric in half. With wrong sides together stitch these two pieces with a ⅝in (1.5cm) seam at each end only leaving a gap ⅞in (2cm) longer than the zip. Tack (baste) the zip opening and press open.

Fold the seam allowance on one piece by ⅜in (1cm) and press it firmly. Place it along the edge of the zip. Pin, tack (baste) and stitch through the fabric and zip.

Open out the fabric with right side facing you and the zip lying flat underneath. Pin, tack (baste) and stitch the second zip edge through all the layers. Remove all tacking (basting) and open the zip.

Machine stitch around the four edges allowing a ⅝in (1.5cm) seam. Trim and finish the seams either with a zigzag or by oversewing.

Turn your cushion to the right side and put your cushion pad through the zip opening.

BOLSTER

To turn your stitched canvas into a bolster all you will require is: lightweight calico; backing fabric; zip; and stuffing or wadding.

To insert the zip, follow the instructions above.

Cut two circles in the backing fabric. Their circumference should be the same as the length of the canvas, and that of the backing fabric, minus the 1¼in (3cm) which has been allowed for the seams.

With wrong sides together, using a ⅝in (1.5cm) seam, sew the canvas and backing fabric together along the long seam. You should now have a tube of fabric. Open the seam and press flat. Open the zip. With right sides together pin, tack (baste) and stitch the circles, one to each end of the tube. Finish the edges.

Turn the cover through the zip opening.

To make a bolster pad to fit your bolster cover cut the calico to the same size as the tube. Sew the long ends together using a ⅝in (1.5cm) seam allowance. Cut two end

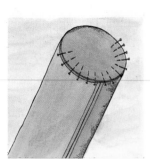

circles. Pin, tack (baste) and stitch one end circle to the tube, with right sides together.

Before fixing the second circle, which will be the other end, fill the tube with stuffing. Make sure it is firmly stuffed. Join the second circle and finish edges.

WALL HANGING

To turn your stitched canvas into a wall hanging you will need: backing fabric (upholstery fabric); 2oz wadding; dowelling rod; and cord or braid.

Cut the edges off the two long sides of the canvas leaving a ⅝in (1.5cm) border. Cut a piece of backing fabric the same size as the canvas.

Cut a piece of wadding slightly smaller than the canvas and tack the wadding to the wrong side of the canvas.

With right sides together sew the backing fabric to the canvas along the side seams. Turn to right side. Turn under ¼in (5mm) at the top and bottom edge. Stitch.

Cut two pieces of dowelling 2in (5cm) longer than the bottom edge of the work. Turn under the top and bottom 1½in (3.5cm). Stitch leaving a gap wide enough to feed the dowelling through. Thread the dowelling through the top and bottom of your work. Attach the cord or braid to each side of the top dowelling rod for hanging.

WAISTCOAT

To make the waistcoat into a garment you will need: fabric for back (a dupion silk is recommended for a really luxurious finish); fabric for lining; buttons; bias strip in lining fabric for piping and rouleaus; and piping cord. You will also need the following pattern pieces: stitched front pieces one left, one right; waistcoat back; pair of front lining pieces; and back lining. Cut fronts from stitched canvas leaving ⅝in (1.5cm) all around each piece. Cut front lining pieces the same size.

Cut back from the pattern on a fold. If you need to adjust the size of the waistcoat add or take in the extra at the centre back. Remember that if you add to the fold to only add half of what you need. Cut the lining to the same size adding an extra ⅞in (2cm) at the centre back. Cut 2in (5cm) wide lengths of bias in the lining fabric joining them together on the cross.

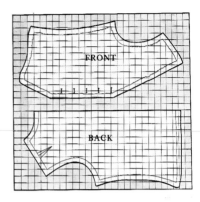

Sew the darts at the shoulders on both the back and the back lining. Sew the front panels to the back, with their right sides together. Then sew the front lining to the back lining, with their right sides together.

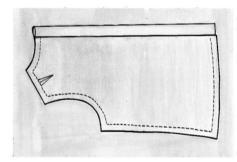

Make a ⅜in (1cm) pleat at the centre back of the lining. Tack it at the top and bottom and press.

Measure around the armhole. Cut two bias strips this length plus 1¼in (3cm). Join them together using a ⅝in (1.5cm) seam. Press the seam open. Attach it right sides together around the armholes. Stagger the seam and turn the bias to the wrong side. Tack (baste) through the waistcoat and the facing on both armholes.

Take a 14in (35.5cm) bias strip and 14in (35.5cm) of piping cord. Turning the end under, hand stitch the bias strip tightly around the cord. Then cut this piped strip into five 2in (5cm) lengths.

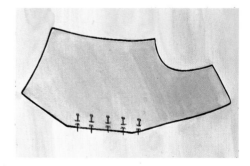

Evenly space five marks along the right-hand side of the centre front, starting below the 'v'. Take each of the piped strips, fold in half and position at these marks, with the raw edges against the centre edge of the waistcoat. Tack (baste) each of these in position.

Measure around the edges and cut a bias strip to this length plus 1¼in (3cm). Cut piping the same length. Fold bias in half around the piping cord. Tack (baste) firmly against the edge of the cord.

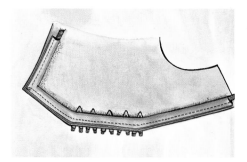

With the piping facing away from the seam, pin, tack and stitch the piped strip all around the edge of the waistcoat.

Turn the seams under so that you can see the piped edges. Trim into the seams and corners so the waistcoat lies flat. Tack (baste) around waistcoat inside seam line, and then press. Turn under ⅝in (1.5cm) around the edge of the lining. Press the lining. Fit the lining to the inside of the waistcoat. Pin, tack (baste) and hand sew in place.

Sew buttons to the left-hand side making sure that they match the position of the buttonholes. Take out any remaining tacking stitches.

MOUNTED PANEL

To turn your stitched canvas into a mounted panel you will need: acid free board; pins; strong thread; and 4oz wadding.

Cut a piece of board slightly larger than the finished needlepoint, and a piece of wadding slightly smaller than this piece of mount board. Place the finished work, right side down, onto a clean, flat surface, with the wadding positioned centrally over the design area. Place the piece of board on top of this.

Turn one long side of the canvas over the board and pin at intervals along the edge making sure that the work is sitting in the middle of the board. Holding the work taut, pin along the opposite edge.

Thread a needle with strong thread. Working from side to side starting at the centre, lace the two edges together. Pull the thread taut.

Repeat this process on the top and bottom edges, folding the corners carefully. Fasten off and finish.

FRAMED PICTURE

To turn your stitched canvas into a framed picture you will need: acid free board; pins; strong thread; 4oz wadding; and a picture mount insert.

Cut a piece of board slightly smaller than the inside of your picture frame and a piece of wadding slightly smaller than the design area of your work.

Place the finished work right side down on to a clean flat surface, with the wadding positioned centrally over the design area. Then place the board on top of this.

Turn one long side of the canvas over the board and pin at intervals along the edge making sure that the work is sitting in the middle of the board. Holding the work taut, pin along the opposite edge.

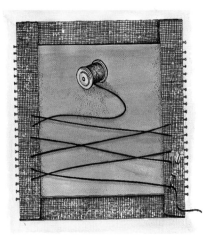

Thread a needle with strong thread. Working from side to side starting at the centre, lace the two edges together. Pull the thread taut. Repeat this process on the remaining edges, folding the corners carefully. and place the mount insert inside the picture frame. Place your work inside the picture frame behind the mount, and fix the backing board into the frame.

AUBUSSON CHAIRSEAT

To complete this project you will need: ⅜in (1cm) tacks; and strong thread.

Leaving 1¾in (4cm) around the edge of the stitched canvas cut the shape for the seat. Make a double row of stitching around the edge of the canvas to reduce fraying. Run a gathering thread around the edge of the canvas, inside the double row. With the stitched piece facing down on a clean surface place the seat pad face down centrally on top. Draw up the gathering thread adjusting the design so it is positioned where you want it on the pad.

Using a hammer, tack the canvas into the hard underside of the pad. Place the pad back on the chair.

CONVERSION CHART

This conversion chart should only be used as a guide
as exact comparisons are not always available.

ANCHOR	DMC	ANCHOR	DMC	ANCHOR	DMC
8002	BLANC	8508	7226	9022	7385
8004	BLANC	8542	7254	9076	7404
8006	ECRU	8542	7260	9078	7406
8012	7745	8542	7459	9080	7428
8020	7484	8542	7790	9214	7362
8040	7472	8546	7264	9256	7422
8054	7739	8588	7711	9274	7584
8058	7504	8604	7244	9282	7679
8060	7455	8608	7243	9324	7493
8060	7506	8610	7243	9324	7724
8162	7360	8686	7798	9382	7491
8168	7946	8714	7284	9382	7492
8196	7606	8714	7292	9384	7724
8204	7107	8792	7306	9386	7463
8220	7110	8820	7802	9388	7513
8234	7875	8824	7296	9388	7525
8258	7124	8824	7591	9392	7514
8258	7851	8824	7930	9394	7416
8264	7169	8838	7288	9402	7492
8264	7447	8838	7297	9442	7452
8306	7851	8882	7327	9442	7453
8366	7760	8882	7701	9446	7174
8368	7196	8894	7692	9448	7174
8368	7354	8896	7323	9504	7171
8368	7759	8898	7927	9524	7918
8400	7758	8904	7339	9602	7448
8400	7961	8906	7999	9622	7840
8412	7202	8924	7860	9674	7624
8414	7204	9002	7542	9678	7234
8418	7205	9020	7541	9768	7624

SUPPLIERS

TAPESTRY WOOLS

Anchor Tapisserie:
Coats Paton Leisure Crafts Group, McMullen Road, Darlington, County Durham DL1 1YQ, England

Susan Bates Inc., P.O. Box F., Route 9A, 212 Middlesex Avenue, Chester, Connecticut 06412, U.S.A.

Appleton Bros. Ltd.:
Thames Works, Church Street, Chiswick, London W4 2PE, England

American Crewel and Canvas Studio, P.O. Box 453, 164 Canal Street, Canastota, Ny 13032, U.S.A.

DMC Creative World:
Pullman Road, Wigston, Leicester LE8 2PY, England

DMC Corporation, Port Kearny Building # 10, South Kearny, New Jersey 07032-0650, U.S.A.

Paterna Ltd.:
P.O. Box 1, Ossett, West Yorkshire WF5 9SA, England

EHRMAN

U.K.:
Ehrman, 14-16 Lancer Square, Kensington Church Street, London W8 4EP

U.S.A.:
Ehrman, 5 Northern Boulevard, Amherst, New Hampshire 03031

Canada:
Pointers, 1017 Mount Pleasant Road, Toronto, Ontario M4P 2MI

Australia:
Tapestry Rose, P.O. Box 366, Canterbury 3126

New Zealand:
Quality Handcrafts, P.O. Box 1486, Auckland

France:
Armada, Collange, Lournand, Cluny 71250

Germany:
Offerta Versand, Brunecker Str. 2a, D–6080 Gross-Gerau

Italy:
Sybilla, D & C S.p.a. Divisione Sybilla, Via Nannetti, 40069 Zola Predosa

Spain:
Canvas and Tapestry, Costanilla de los Angeles 2, 28013 Madrid

Belgium and Holland:
Hedera, Diestsestraat 172, 3000 Leuven

Switzerland:
Bopp Interieur AG, Postrasse 1, CH - 8001 Zurich

Sweden:
Wincent, Svearvagen 94, 113 50 Stockholm

Finland:
Novita, P.O. Box 59, 00211 Helsinki

Denmark:
Designer Garn, Vesterbro 33A, DK 9000 Aalborg

Iceland:
Storkurinn, Kjorgardi, Laugavegi 159, 101 Reykjavik

Argentina:
Vickimport SA, 25 de Mayo 596, Sp, (1002) Buenos Aires

143

ACKNOWLEDGEMENTS

Thanks to:	For:
Vivienne Wells	Commissioning the book
Brenda Morrison	Art direction
Zöe and Tim Hill	Some great pictures
Carole Keegan	Typing skills
Ethan Danielson	Sorting out the charts
Nic Barlow	Portrait photography
David & Charles	Footing the bill
Ruth Gill Interiors 15 Topsfield Parade, London N8 8PU Tel: 0181 340 6300	Chaise longue, vase, stand candelabra and yellow cushions on page 26

And special thanks to:	For:
Kaffe Fassett	A partnership of nearly twenty years, building this business

INDEX